W9-CLE-370

Economic Rights and Environmental Wrongs

Economic Rights and Environmental Wrongs

Property Rights for the Common Good

Rose Anne Devlin and R. Quentin Grafton

Department of Economics
University of Ottawa

Edward Elgar
Cheltenham, UK • Northampton, MA, USA

Published by
Edward Elgar Publishing Limited
8 Lansdown Place
Cheltenham
Glos GL50 2HU
UK

Edward Elgar Publishing, Inc.
6 Market Street
Northampton
Massachusetts 01060
USA

A catalogue record for this book
is available from the British Library

Library of Congress Cataloguing-in-Publication Data
Devlin, Rose Anne, 1956–
    Economic rights and environmental wrongs : property rights for the
common good / Rose Anne Devlin, R. Quentin Grafton.
    Includes bibliographical references and index.
    1. Environmental degradation—Economic aspects. 2. Environmental
economics. 3. Right of property. 4. environmental responsibility.
I. Grafton, R. Quentin, 1962– . II. Title.
GE140.D48 1998
363.7'058—dc21   97-33596
                                                                             CIP

ISBN 1 85898 450 5

Printed and bound in Great Britain by
MPG Books Ltd, Bodmin, Cornwall

To Thomas, and Brecon and Ariana
May they inherit a better world

Department of Economics
PO Box 450, Station A
Ottawa, Ontario
Canada
K1N 6N5
(613) 562-5800 Ext. 1432 and 1688
Fax (613) 562-5999
radevlin@uottawa.ca
qgrafton@uottawa.ca

Contents

List of Figures

Preface

When we read newspapers or magazines, listen to the radio or watch the television we are likely to learn about at least one environmental challenge or crisis every week. If it is not a global problem like the depletion of the ozone layer, it is a regional concern over acid rain or even a local question of how to find a suitable site for a nearby town's landfill. The fact that you're now reading *Economic Rights and Environmental Wrongs* means that you are certainly aware of many of these challenges. You are concerned about the problems of pollution, and the fact that many natural resources, such as fish, forests and farming land, are not being used as they should be. Our book provides a way to understand how these problems arise.

Economic Rights and Environmental Wrongs describes a simple but powerful framework for understanding the causes of environmental challenges whether they be global warming, smog, species loss, deforestation, the collapse of fish stocks or the disposal of nuclear wastes. In many cases, the over exploitation of natural resources and the degradation of the environment arise because the characteristics of ownership are such that people, firms and communities do not bear the full cost of their actions. This is true when someone drops litter in a city park or when a firm discharges its wastes into a river without considering the consequences. Forcing individuals and companies to consider the costs of pollution and misuse of natural resources is an important step to remedying environmental problems. We show how creating and enforcing property rights can provide the incentives for people to change their behaviour, leading to an improved and well-managed environment.

Our book will be of interest to casual readers as well as to students of various disciplines like environmental economics, environmental studies, environmental science, ecology, geography, biology, forestry, fisheries, agriculture and anthropology. To make the ideas accessible to all readers we assume no prior knowledge of economics or environmental science. If you understand *Economic Rights and Environmental Wrongs* we believe that you will not only appreciate the world's major environmental challenges, but will also have a framework to analyse what can be done to help address them. To explore these issues, we use many examples and cases from around the world to illustrate the causes of environmental problems and how property rights may remedy them. These examples and cases provide a unique and practical source of information on such topics as biodiversity, the depletion of the ozone layer, and deforestation.

The book consists of six parts: Chapter 1 sets out the environmental challenges we face; Chapter 2 sketches a framework for understanding the underlying causes of pollution; Chapter 3 shows how private property rights, if appropriately applied, can mitigate the problems of pollution and environmental degradation; Chapter 4 provides a structure for understanding property rights and examines how they can be used to help overcome many natural resource problems like tropical deforestation, over exploitation of fisheries, and species extinction; Chapter 5 describes alternative approaches to addressing environmental challenges; and Chapter 6 synthesizes the important concepts discussed throughout the book.

Important features of the book include suggestions for further reading located at the back of each chapter, a list of useful World Wide Web sites on environmental issues, and a detailed glossary of environmental and economic terms located at the back of the book. All words in the text in italics are defined in the glossary. The further readings open doors to a broad range of perspectives on the environment and a variety of topics ranging from global warming to sustainable development. The views expressed do not always coincide with our own. Nevertheless, we believe it is worthwhile to provide a reading list that reflects the range of perspectives that exists in the literature. Unlike some of the books in the further readings, we do believe that economics offers a useful framework to help understand and solve our environmental challenges. We hope that when you finish reading *Economic Rights and Environmental Wrongs* you will reach the same conclusion.

R.A.D. and R.Q.G.

Ottawa, Canada

Acknowledgements

We owe a great debt to the many people who have contributed to our understanding of the environment, economics, and property rights. We especially recognize the insights of Tony Scott. Most of all we acknowledge the support and encouragement of our spouses, Dane and Carol-Anne. To all of you who helped us along the way, thank you!

We thank Johnny Abedrabbo for assistance in the production of figures and graphs and Milan Jayasinghe for research assistance and for helping us to produce a camera-ready copy of our manuscript.

1

Environmental Wrongs

1.1   HARM, HISTORY AND HUMANITY

From just a handful of individuals a hundred thousand years ago, humanity will number over 6 billion by the year 2000 and is increasing at the rate of 250,000 people a day. Every month we add to the world's population a city the size of Paris and almost all of this increase takes place in just 16 countries in Africa, Latin America and Asia. This rapid rise in population is occurring alongside a dramatic increase in the consumption of all types of goods and services. Not surprisingly, our environment is changing at a rate that would have seemed impossible just two or three generations ago.

With a few exceptions, many wild populations of species and their habitats have diminished in size from just a few decades ago. Indeed, some important wild populations which have sustained us for generations - such as fisheries - have collapsed and hundreds of animal species are in danger of extinction. We are losing tropical forest at a rapid rate and hundreds of millions of people live or work in environments harmful to their health. Not so long ago, the suggestion that humans could cause global climate change or that schoolchildren would be advised to stay indoors for protection during periods of intense sunlight, would have been viewed as science fiction.

The fact that humans affect the environment is not new. The practices of some prehistoric hunting societies may well have hastened the extinction of some large temperate animals like the woolly mammoth. The arrival of humans in North America some 20,000 years ago coincided with a massive disappearance of animal species (Martin, 1967). Later arrivals of humans in

1

Madagascar about 1,500 years ago and New Zealand 1,000 years ago also led to major environmental changes. Even before the Roman Empire, when the earth's population was no more than 3 per cent of what it is today, large areas of the Mediterranean were deforested and changed by human activity.

From the first domestication of animals some 10,000 years ago and the planting of crops, humans have had a major impact on natural resources. Sometimes the destruction of local environments has had devastating effects on human populations. Strong evidence suggests, for instance, that the collapse of many Mayan cities came about because the environment was unable to support their populations. Deforestation is the likely cause of the collapse of the highly sophisticated farming towns of the thirteenth century Anastazi in the American southwest while the sixteenth century fall of Great Zimbabwe, in the country which bears its name, is attributed to overgrazing combined with climate change.

Environmental change shapes our history as well as the physical world. Mass migrations in the Mediterranean and Middle East, triggered by environmental factors over three thousand years ago, contributed to the collapse of the Minoan and Hittite civilizations. More recently, the colonization of the Americas, Southern Africa and Australasia was caused by the search for more abundant resources - especially agricultural land by Europeans.

Despite the relationship between the size of the human population and the use of the environment and natural resources, it is **how** we use the earth's resources which ultimately determines the state of the world. More people does not necessarily mean a worse environment. We have the ability to be informed about the consequences of our actions in a way unimaginable 50 years ago. And, as is detailed throughout this book, we can create the right incentives and institutions to make individuals, businesses and communities pay the cost of their actions. The consequences of not caring for ourselves and our planet are all too clear.

The World Writ Small?

The negative effects of human activity on the environment is exemplified by the settlement of Easter Island. Its first inhabitants were Polynesians, probably numbering no more than 50 to 100 people, who arrived from the western Pacific by canoe around 400 AD. They discovered a fertile land blessed with a subtropical climate covered in a mixed forest of palms and other trees, bushes and ferns. For meat, the islanders enjoyed fish, sea and land birds, porpoises caught some distance offshore, and rats and chickens which they brought with them. For plants, the islanders grew typical Polynesian crops such as taro, sweet potatoes and bananas.

Archaeological records show that by 800 AD a significant area of land was no longer forested, having been cleared and replaced by grassland. The process of deforestation continued as its population burgeoned. The decline in the erection of the statues, for which Easter Island remains famous, coincided with the demise and extinction of the Easter Island palm tree which provided the means for the hauling and manoeuvring of heads which weighed as much as 82 tons. Shortly after 1400 AD, the last palm tree on the island was felled. This was to have an important impact on the islanders not just in terms of statue construction but because the loss of large trees meant that the islanders could not make sea-worthy canoes. In turn, this prevented the islanders from supplementing their diets with the porpoises that had represented a substantial part of their food.

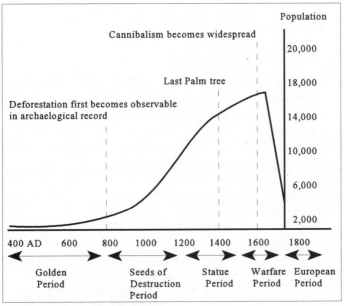

Figure 1.1   Easter Island

The depletion of the island's resource base, and an unsustainable population that may have been as high as 20,000 at its peak, left the islanders with few options. Conflict over the limited resources led to a breakdown in the traditional governing structure, and widespread warfare between rival groups took place during the seventeenth and eighteenth centuries. Over this period, cannibalism appears to have become widespread, with evidence of malnutrition and perhaps even starvation. By the time the first Europeans found Easter Island in 1722, it was described as having a "...wasted appearance [which] could give no other impression than of singular poverty and barrenness" (Diamond, 1995, p. 64). The destruction of natural resources clearly coincided with a rapid fall in the human population. The history of Easter Island is depicted in Figure 1.1.

Some people view Easter Island as a stark example of what may happen to the world if we do not change the way we use the environment. Fortunately, humanity as a whole now has the power to shape its own future in ways that were not available to the Easter Islanders.

1.2   THE ENVIRONMENTAL CHALLENGE

Land

One of the greatest environmental challenges facing land today concerns how to stop the problems of soil *erosion* and degradation. The crops which feed us, or the animals we husband, all require soils. Soils are not rocks which can be mined but are, in a sense, a renewable resource as long as they are nurtured and managed properly. Just as plants need soil to grow, soil fertility is a function of its organic matter, micro and macro nutrients, and the crops cultivated. Without soil, life as we know it would not exist. In fact, a decline in soil fertility and soil degradation has been responsible for the fall of entire civilizations and cultures.

Despite the importance of maintaining soil fertility, in many parts of the world soils are being denuded at a faster rate than they are being formed. In the United States, the average rate of erosion may be as much as seven times higher than the rate of soil formation. China's Gansu province has one of the highest rates of soil erosion in the world; soil loss as much as 30 tons per hectare has been recorded in its Loess Plateau. Soil erosion, accelerated by human activity, is responsible for washing an incredible 1.6 billion tons of soil and debris a year into the Yellow River. An even greater amount is thought to be transported in the Ganges. Although soil loss can, to some extent, be compensated for by applying fertilizers or using other inputs, it does result in lower yields than otherwise. By one estimate, about 10 per cent of the earth's cultivated land has moderate or worse soil degradation as a result of human activity (Oldeman *et al.*, 1990). Soil erosion and degradation from farming and overgrazing also contribute to *desertification*.

Soils are also affected by *salinization*, or the accumulation of salts which can occur when evaporation exceeds precipitation in arid areas, by the depletion of water tables, and by irrigation. One estimate suggests as much as a quarter of all irrigated land suffers, at least to some extent, from salinization. Tropical areas suffer from another major soil problem called *laterization*. In this problem, cultivation or deforestation result in metal oxides being released from the soil, significantly reducing its fertility. As a result, the productivity of agricultural land diminishes and, combined with urban expansion, the area available for agriculture is reduced which limits our potential to produce food. Dealing with soil erosion and degradation poses a formidable challenge for society, and one that is of critical importance to hundreds of millions of people.

Another challenge we face is deforestation. Most of the loss of forests takes place in just four countries: Brazil, India, Indonesia and Colombia. These countries are depleting their forests just like Europeans and North Americans did in the past - to sell or use the wood and to increase the area of land under cultivation or pasture. However, a problem arises because tropical forests provide a number of benefits to **all** humankind. Growing forests represent an important *carbon sink* by absorbing more carbon dioxide that they emit, and thus may slow down the global climate change that is thought to arise with greenhouse gas emissions. Tropical forests also provide a home for about a quarter of the world's species; their destruction will reduce biological diversity. Biodiversity is important for a number of reasons not the least of which is that it gives us options to improve crops through genetic engineering and the use of hybrids of wild and domestic varieties of plants, and because biodiversity can help us to develop cures for diseases. The destruction of tropical habitats may also expose us to previously unknown pathogens - such as the deadly Ebola virus - that may live in creatures that previously have had limited contact with humans. Further, deforestation can erode and denude soils. For example, along the Tapajos River, a tributary of the Amazon, the cutting and burning of trees has resulted in the loss of 15 to 30 centimetres of surface soil. In turn, this releases naturally occurring mercury in the soil which has contributed to high levels of mercury in the people who eat the fish from the local streams and rivers.

The disposal of wastes poses another important environmental concern. Every year millions of tonnes of waste are produced. If handled and treated properly, most of this waste can have a limited impact on the environment. Unfortunately, the treating and disposal of wastes - especially hazardous wastes

- can be very expensive. This creates incentives for individuals, firms and even governments to dispose of them improperly. In most of the industrialized world, organic wastes are treated and do not represent a major health threat; however, this is not the case in many developing countries where parasites and gastrointestinal infections dramatically reduce life expectancy and represent a major cause of infant mortality. Indeed, in some cities in developing countries a significant proportion of the solid wastes are not even collected for disposal - more than two thirds in Karachi and almost four fifths in Dar es Salaam (World Bank, 1992) - reducing both the quality of life and standards of health.

In richer countries, the improper disposal of industrial and city wastes generates the most concern. Organic chemicals such as polychlorinated biphenyls (PCBs) are particularly worrisome because, among other things, they have been linked to male sterility in mammals. Concentrations of heavy metals such as mercury, lead and cadmium in the environment have been linked to various ailments, including cancer. Even in countries with very stringent controls on the disposal of such wastes, like the United States, there are many examples of improper disposal. For example, the small community of Times Beach, Missouri had waste oil sprayed to keep the dust down on its dirt roads. Unfortunately, this oil had been mixed with toxic chemicals and led to very high levels of dioxin in the soil - a chemical that has been linked to soft-tissue cancers at high levels of exposure (Chiras, 1994, p. 462).

The proper disposal of nuclear wastes represents another important environmental issue. One way to store these wastes - which can be radioactive for thousands of years - safely is to bury them deep in the earth's surface. The problem here is to find geological strata, not prone to seismic or other disturbances, which can minimize contamination should the containers holding the waste leak. Nuclear testing poses a further environmental concern. Despite a partial ban on atmospheric testing, France continued such tests in the South Pacific into the 1970s. Underground testing, which limits most of the fallout to a well-defined area, is also problematic for people who live near the test sites. A fear of radiation leaks is also shared by people who live close to nuclear power stations. Although there have been very few large-scale nuclear accidents, the Three Mile Island incident in 1979 illustrates the potential hazards associated with nuclear power generation, and the 1986 Chernobyl accident shows how a meltdown can lead to a fallout thousands of kilometres away. The Chernobyl accident to date has led to 350 deaths and may well result in the premature death of at least 10,000 people (Pickering and Owen, 1994).

The costs of dealing with hazardous wastes have led, in some cases, to their export from rich to poor countries where they are frequently disposed of improperly. Some countries have even received wastes illegally such as when

400,000 litres of hazardous materials were found dumped on the ground in Tecate, Mexico or when 3,800 tonnes of mixed chemical and industrial waste from Europe were illegally disposed of in Koko, Nigeria (Elliott, 1994).

Agricultural production also generates problems with run-off from the chemically-fertilized land and disposal of animal wastes. The high use of artificial fertilizers on farm land increases the levels of nitrates in rivers, lakes and aquifers, reducing water quality and potentially leading to excessive plant and algae growth. Furthermore, some pesticides - such as DDT - can lead to genetic and other health problems for animals high up in the food chain.

Water

Ensuring the availability of clean, safe drinking water poses a major environmental challenge. For people who are used to turning on a tap and quenching their thirst it may be hard to imagine that hundreds of millions of people do not have adequate access to potable water for drinking or safe water for bathing. In Haiti, one of the poorest countries in the western hemisphere, a little over half the population in urban areas and only about a third of the population in rural areas have access to safe drinking water (World Bank, 1994a). These proportions are not atypical for the world's poorest countries; in Mali less than 5 per cent of the rural populace have safe, potable water. Poor quality water in low-income countries is a result of poverty. Poverty means that less money is available to be spent on infrastructure - such as piping water from wells or disposing of sewage properly.

In richer countries, the environmental challenge is to use water resources wisely. The diversion of water from rivers for agricultural projects and hydroelectric power generation has important effects on the environment. The tragedy of the Aral Sea in the Russian Federation, which has been reduced to about one third of its former volume due to the diversion of two rivers for irrigation, illustrates the potential damages arising from the mismanagement of water resources. Other problems include changes to local climates, the destruction of fisheries and wildlife, and soil erosion and salinization. Megaprojects which divert or dam large bodies of water bring with them special problems. The Three Gorges project on China's Yangtze River will displace up to 1.5 million people and submerge the Xiling, Wu and Qutang gorges which include some of the most spectacular scenery in the world. The diversion of water flows can also have a negative effect on wetlands and estuaries that are very important ecosystems, especially for bird life.

The challenge facing some countries is that water consumption exceeds its replenishment. In the western United States, many farmers depend on irrigation to grow their crops. Unfortunately, a significant proportion of this water is being drawn from aquifers at a faster rate than it is being replaced. The depletion of water tables is also occurring in important agricultural areas of India and China. In the Middle East, access to scarce water resources is an important environmental, economic and political problem.

Challenges concerning water resources go beyond the use of rivers, lakes and aquifers. Air pollution from emissions of sulphur dioxide is causing significant damage in Scandinavia and eastern North America. In the Adirondacks in New York State, one in ten lakes has a pH of less than 6.0. As a result some fish, like smallmouth bass, and insect species, like mayfly, are not able to survive. In three quarters of these lakes this problem is attributed to acid rain (Kulp, 1995). In addition, the deposition of pollutants from the air has also been a major factor affecting the water quality of the Great Lakes - an area where 40 million people live. Lake Erie has been the worst affected but even Lake Superior - the largest and cleanest of the five great lakes - receives thousands of tons of pollutants, such as aluminium, phosphates and PCBs every year. Water pollution also arises from the contamination of aquifers and supplies of drinking water. Potential health hazards include increased rates of certain types of cancer.

More obvious forms of water pollution include the discharge of sewage and other wastes in rivers and oceans. One of the most famous cases occurred in Minamata Bay, southwestern Japan, with the discharge of inorganic mercury by a chemical plant. This mercury changed into methyl mercury and was absorbed by the fish and their predators, including people. By 1960 more than a 100 people were diagnosed with *Minamata Disease* which affects the central nervous system. Of these people, some 20 per cent died from the disease and by 1987 over 1,700 people were diagnosed with mercury poisoning (Kudo and Miyahara, 1992). Unfortunately, similar incidents have also occurred elsewhere. In 1970, it was discovered that a pulp and paper mill near Dryden in Canada had discharged several tons of mercury into a river system used by natives as an important source of fish and food.

The direct dumping of sewage and hazardous wastes into oceans is also of concern. One example is the disposal of low-level nuclear waste at sea by the Sellafield nuclear plant in England. In 1983, the British government issued a public health warning to persons using a 50 kilometre stretch of the English coast after it was found that parts of it had been contaminated with radioactive waste discharged by the Sellafield plant. In some cases, the contamination registered 1,000 times greater than normal. Marine pollution has also arisen from oil slicks such as occurred with the 1989 *Exxon Valdez* disaster in Alaska or the *Amoco Cadiz* which struck France's Brittany coast in 1987 discharging

223,000 tons of oil and contaminating 300 kilometres of coastline (Pickering and Owen, 1994, p. 150).

Environmental concerns over ocean resources go far beyond marine pollution and oil spills. There are millions of people who directly or indirectly earn their living from fishing, and many who depend on fish for protein. Although fisheries are subject to natural fluctuations and changes in population, there is no question that over fishing has severely damaged some fish stocks. The most dramatic downturn has been in the Peruvian anchoveta which used to be the world's largest fishery. In 1971 the total annual catch was some 10.25 million tons yet just two years later it had fallen to 1.75 million tons. Canada's Atlantic cod fisheries have been harvested since the sixteenth century yet it was only in the past two decades that over exploitation led to a collapse of the fisheries. From a total catch of over 500,000 tons in the 1980s, almost all the cod fisheries are currently under a fishing moratorium to help the fish stocks recover (Grafton, 1996c).

Air

Air pollution, in one form or another, affects our local and global environment. Emissions in the form of greenhouse gases (carbon dioxide, methane, nitrous oxides) may be leading to global climate warming while the use of chlorofluorocarbons (CFCs) and halons have also contributed to a thinning of the stratospheric ozone layer which protects the earth from ultraviolet-B radiation. Every day millions of people live and work in cities where poor air quality affects their health.

Global warming is one of the most widely-discussed environmental challenges of the day. However, as early as the nineteenth century some scientists warned that increasing the amount of carbon dioxide in the atmosphere would increase the average temperature of the world. In fact, since 1800 the concentration of carbon dioxide in the atmosphere has risen by over 25 per cent. Over the same period, levels of methane (11 times greater potential for global warming per molecule than carbon dioxide) have more than doubled. If present trends continue, the concentration of carbon dioxide, which accounts for about the three quarters of the global warming potential from all greenhouse gases, may double by the end of next century.

While the exact effect of greenhouse gases on global temperatures is subject to debate, estimates of the increase in average temperature range from about one half a degree Celsius to as much as five degrees Celsius, depending upon the model, assumptions, and time horizon used. To put this in perspective, the earth's average temperature has increased by about one half a degree Celsius since the middle of the nineteenth century. Although the regional effects are difficult to predict, some areas of the world will likely become drier and others wetter, weather extremes such as tornadoes and hurricanes may become more frequent, and the sea-level - due to thermal expansion - would almost certainly increase, perhaps by as much as 0.75 to 1 metre. And, if global warming were to melt the Antarctic ice cap - considered by many scientists to be extremely unlikely - the sea could rise as much as 55 metres! However, the environmental challenge from global warming is not just how much the average temperature increases but at what rate. A slow rate of change will help us to adapt the crops we grow and put flood control measures in place. Although the largest changes in temperature are expected to be in the middle and temperate latitudes, the greatest challenge may be faced by poorer tropical countries. Worldwide, hundreds of million of people live on flood plains or low-lying areas and many more depend on the arrival of monsoons at specific times of the year. The consequences for the poor of a country like Bangladesh from increases in the sea level of almost a metre would be very serious, as would be the failure of the monsoons to arrive on time.

The other global atmospheric challenge we face is the thinning of the ozone layer which shields the earth from harmful ultraviolet radiation. The amount of ozone in the stratosphere is not constant. Naturally occurring changes are hypothesized to be a function of fluctuations in sea-surface temperatures - especially in the eastern Pacific ocean. However, the CFCs and halons released into the atmosphere eventually react with ozone (O_3) molecules and reduce the levels of stratospheric ozone. A significant decline of ozone between altitudes of 12 to 22 kilometres in Antarctica was reported by British scientists in a paper published in 1985. Subsequent observations in Antarctica have revealed that upper level ozone in the Antarctic has continued to decrease and in 1991 was 10 to 15 per cent less than recorded in previous years. Depletion of stratospheric ozone is also occurring in northern latitudes with levels falling by as much as 10 per cent at 30 degrees north between 1979 and 1990.

The potential consequences of the depletion of stratospheric ozone include higher rates of skin cancer, cataracts, and a reduced immune response. It may also have unfavourable effects on animal and plant populations. One estimate suggests that a one per cent decline in stratospheric ozone will lead to a two per cent increase in surface ultraviolet radiation. Unless people reduce their exposure to sunlight, especially at times of high intensity ultraviolet radiation, this same reduction in ozone may eventually result in a two per cent increase in skin cancers (Titus, 1986).

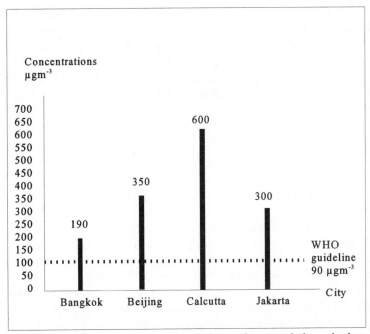

Figure 1.2 Annual mean concentrations of suspended particulate matter, 1990. Source: UNEP, 1992.

Perhaps the most noticeable environmental problem is local air pollution. More than a billion people live or work in cities with an unacceptable level (as defined by the World Health Organization) of suspended particulate matter and sulphur dioxide (World Bank, 1992). In some cities, such as Bangkok, Beijing, Calcutta and Jakarta the levels of suspended particulate matter in the air exceed the maximum World Health Organization (WHO) guidelines more than 200 days a year. A comparison of the air pollution in these cities relative to the maximum guidelines of the WHO is given in Figure 1.2.

The consequences of air pollution on morbidity and mortality are significant. People with pulmonary and coronary diseases are particularly at risk, as are children. According to one estimate, between 300,000 and 700,0000 premature deaths would be avoided (World Bank, 1992) if developing countries met the WHO guidelines for suspended particulate matter. Leaded gasoline, which has been eliminated in most rich and industrialized countries, also contributes to lead poisoning in affected populations. High lead concentrations have been linked to neurological problems and reduced intelligence. In some places, such as Mexico City, almost a third of all children have elevated levels of lead in their bodies. These problems are compounded by indoor air pollution, which comes from inhaling smoke from fires used in cooking and heating. Indoor smoke is a major contributor to acute respiratory infections which kill about 4 million children and infants every year. Air pollution, in the form of ground level ozone and sulphur dioxide, also contributes to crop losses and can negatively affect trees and forests.

1.3   HUMANITY AND THE ENVIRONMENT

The list of environmental problems - local and global - provides a sobering perspective on the challenges that we face. Whether the problems be pollution or the over exploitation of natural resources, humanity has had an important and negative impact on many ecosystems. Although the human species has not yet reached the environmental limits faced by the Easter Islanders, we do need to adjust our behaviour, production and consumption so that future generations have the potential to enjoy a quality of life as least as good as our own.

Contrary to the popular belief of some people, a change for the better will not take place by leaving habitats "forever wild", stopping all population growth or by going "back to nature ". Very few habitats are unaffected by humans. In a sense the "wilderness", whether we like it or not, is what we make it. Even in the vast Amazon rainforest, humans were burning down trees thousands of years ago. Before Columbus arrived in the Americas, most of the eastern United States was managed by the repeated burn-off of vegetation by Native Americans; large areas of land along the lower stretches of the Mississippi River were under cultivation. Much of California, which was previously thought to be in a "natural state" prior to the arrival of the Spanish, had in fact been managed with burn-offs for centuries to increase the incidence of oaks and the production of acorns. If "back to nature" means relying exclusively on organic farming and forsaking the technology of a modern industrial society we simply cannot hope to address our environmental problems. Without developments in plant breeding and the technological breakthroughs which led to the widespread use of higher yielding varieties of rice and other grains in the *green revolution*, food production would not have kept pace with the human population in the past 30 years. Food for thought for the hundreds of millions of people who rely on the grain they produce to survive.

Humankind, while at the root of many of the environmental challenges we face, also holds the key to environmental progress. Altering how people produce and consume - the ultimate cause of our environmental challenges - requires inducing individuals to behave such that their self interest coincides with the public interest. An important way to achieve this goal is to provide individuals and communities with rights over resources and with control over their environment. With property rights, individuals must pay to degrade the environment. In turn, this cost alters individual behaviour and results in fewer environmental problems. It is no coincidence that some of the world's most polluted places are in countries where individual and community rights have frequently been given little thought.

Dealing with environmental problems also involves solving human problems. In many countries, people are so poor that they can neither invest in nor consider the future. For example, by forgoing consumption today, farmers in Haiti - a country severely affected by soil erosion - could control hillside erosion by planting trees and grasses and/or terracing. However, if these farmers do not have enough to eat today they can hardly be expected to be concerned about tomorrow.

Solving global environmental problems also requires global cooperation and action. A country which limits or reduces its emissions of greenhouse gases will have little effect on potential global warming without similar action by other nations. For cooperation to be successful, the costs and benefits of improving the global environment must be shared so that most nations benefit. For example, if conserving tropical forests, so as to maintain biological diversity, is important to temperate, high-income countries then they must be prepared to share the benefits of biodiversity with the countries in which the tropical forests are located.

1.4   RIGHTS AND REMEDIES

Although environmental problems constitute a major concern, they are not an inevitable side effect of humanity. Countries which have had increases in both population and economic activity have experienced improvements in their environment. For example, in the past 25 years, the economic output of most western industrialized countries has risen by over 50 per cent yet the quality of many of their environments has also improved. The United States has seen a dramatic decline in the total emissions of lead and carbon monoxide, and levels of total suspended particulates are less than half what they were in the 1940s (Ellsaesser, 1995). London, at one point known for the poor quality of its air, is now a much healthier place than a generation ago.

Many habitats in Europe and North America, valued for their beauty or the uniqueness of their ecosystem, have come under some form of protection in the past 40 years which limits or excludes exploitation. Worldwide, almost 3 million additional square kilometres were placed in protected status from 1975 to the late 1980s (Sedjo, 1995). The disposal of both industrial and organic wastes is also much improved compared to the 1970s, as is our ability to detect toxins in the environment. Energy conservation and the recycling of consumer wastes has also improved, as has the technology to control and limit emissions in many industrial processes.

These improvements in environmental quality have been almost universally welcomed by people in the industrialized world. They have come about, in large part, by the imposition of enforceable regulations and standards, by changes in technology, by forcing people and firms to pay for the cost of their actions, and by the assignment of property rights. For example, due to standards set by governments, automobiles made in the United States today produce only about one per cent of the emissions of cars built before 1970, and require less than one half the fuel per kilometre. International cooperation has virtually eliminated the production of CFCs which should return stratospheric ozone levels to their natural state by 2040 (Easterbrook, 1995, p. 538). After years of increasing deforestation, the early 1990s have witnessed a sharp decline in the loss of Brazilian rainforest due, in part, to the removal of subsidies to convert forests into farm and ranch land (Andersen *et al.*, 1996). Rising incomes in developing countries may also, eventually, lead to other improvements in the environment (Forrest, 1995) - especially if incentives are introduced so that private interests coincide with social interests.

Given enlightened policies, many poorer countries could improve the standard of living of their citizens as well as the overall quality of their environments. This progress, however, will not take place by exhorting people to change their value systems, by "stopping the clock" in terms of material development or by leaving all environments in their "natural state". It will also not happen by chance with some invisible hand or by inevitable technological progress that will solve all of humanity's problems. Environmental challenges will be met because people have the self-interest to make it happen. Creating the right mix of incentives and controls, therefore, is probably one of the most important tasks the world faces.

One of the big hurdles in the way of setting adequate policies is the lack of detailed information about the state of the world, and uncertainty about our impact on it. Twenty years ago a major worry of some climatologists and environmentalists was that the earth was cooling and that another ice age may start. Today, we worry about global warming. Although biological diversity is crucial, surprisingly we don't even know the number of species on earth or how many disappear as a result of human activities. Further examples of the need for basic information include our ignorance of the effects of atmospheric pollution on global warming and estimates of rainforest damage. In 1988, for instance, rainforest loss in the Amazon was estimated by one researcher to be as much as 162,000 square kilometres. However, updated estimates put the loss at about 20,000 square kilometres (Fearnside, 1990). In the early 1980s many people believed that sulphur dioxide was a greenhouse gas, albeit a minor one. In fact, it tends to have a cooling effect in terms of the earth's temperature. A lack of information does not mean, however, that we should not set up policies or actions to address environmental problems. If we know that tropical forests have a value over and above their worth as timber it makes little sense to subsidize or pay people to convert them into farmland even if we cannot estimate their value in terms of biodiversity. If a factory emits nitrous oxide into the air which affects air quality it should pay for its actions even if we cannot determine exactly what is the cost to the environment.

Wherever possible, policies for sustainable development should provide people with incentives to act in a desirable way. Ordering or forcing people to behave in a particular way may not be very effective especially where few alternatives exist and enforcement of such rules is very limited. For instance, prohibitions against the hunting of wildlife in some African game reserves and national parks may be counterproductive because the costs of enforcement are so high relative to the returns. An incentive-based approach which gives people in or near the parks a share of tourist revenues and/or the right to undertake controlled hunts may be both cheaper and more effective at preserving habitat and wildlife.

Ensuring that people face the right incentives often involves supplying them with either a long-term interest or a property right for natural resources. Environments which are treated as free to all are typically poorly managed and degraded. Establishing property rights over natural resources is an important step in addressing this environmental challenge. Property rights can help achieve a world where the benefits and costs of using the environment are given equal weight, a world where we recognize natural limits, and where future generations have the opportunity to be as well off as we are today.

1.5   FURTHER READING

There is a huge literature on the environment that encompasses all perspectives from doomsday scenarios - the end of the world is near - to Star Trek - the belief that technology will solve all of our problems. For an interesting, if somewhat depressing, view of the world's environmental problems we recommend the annual volumes published by the Worldwatch Institute since 1984 entitled *State of the World.* These publications are designed to inform policy makers about the human impact on the environment and focus on declines in environmental quality. Well-researched descriptions of the world's resources and state of the environment are available from the World Resources Institute (www.wri.org). A pessimistic view of the health of our planet is offered by Goodland (1992) and Brown (1995) who argue that the world has already reached its biological limits. A more optimistic view of the world is found in *The True State of the Planet* (1995), a volume of 10 essays on the environment, and *The State of Humanity* (1995) which is a collection of 58 contributions on topics ranging from global warming to species loss. Differing viewpoints on whether we do or do not face an environmental crisis in terms of pesticide use, waste disposal, and air and water pollution is provided by Bernards (1991). Duraiappah (1996) reviews the literature and provides an overview of environmental degradation in the air, water and land from a property rights perspective. Stern *et al.* (1996) examine the relationship between economic growth and environmental degradation.

Comprehensive books on global environmental issues include Pickering and Owen (1994) and Chiras (1994) while Allaby (1996) provides a nice introduction to environmental science. Somerville (1996) examines from a scientific perspective the human impact on the atmosphere. A very nice overview on the issues of development and the environment is provided by the World Bank (1992). An historical perspective on nature in the United States and South Africa is given by Beinart and Coates (1995) while Simmons (1993) provides an easy-to-read review of environmental history. Ponting (1991), chapter nine, gives a very sobering view of the human potential to affect ecosystems. An introduction to what happened on Easter Island is discussed by Diamond (1995) and in chapter one of Ponting (1991).

Easterbrook (1995) provides a very readable review of the major environmental challenges from the viewpoint of an "ecorealist". Baarschers (1996) provides the essential facts to better understand many of the debates on the environment including the effect of CFCs on stratospheric ozone, toxins and cancer, and air and water quality from the perspective of a chemist. We also highly recommend Goudie (1994) and Nisbet (1991) for an understanding of the effects of human activity on the global environment.

Two thought-provoking books on environmentalism and managing nature are Kaufman (1994) and Budiansky (1995). A review of sustainable development is given by Pearce *et al.* (1990) and an easy-to-read introduction is supplied by Elliott (1994). Bromley (1991) provides the theory and Panayotou (1993) some examples of how to use property rights to address environmental issues. A free market approach to environmentalism is presented by Anderson and Leal (1991). An overview of what environmental economics has to offer in terms of the environmental challenges we face is given by Cropper and Oates (1992).

To appreciate the difficulties in making predictions about the environment, we recommend reading the contribution by Baumol and Oates (Appendix A) in *The State of Humanity*. The errors in prediction, even with complicated computer models, are evident in Meadows *et al.* (1972).

2

Externalities and the Environment

2.1 EXTERNALITIES

The problems of the destruction of the ozone layer, global warming or even the noise from a neighbour's lawnmower on an early Sunday morning are called *externalities*. They arise whenever individuals or firms act without considering their impact on others. Externalities exist in many forms: they are "positive" when people's actions benefit others, and "negative" when they do not. Our focus in this book is on negative externalities. For example, if my sleep is disturbed early on Sunday morning by my neighbour mowing his lawn, a negative externality has occurred because my neighbour doesn't consider the consequences of his actions on my sleep. If I value sleep more than he values mowing the lawn early on Sunday, we do not have a socially desirable outcome because it is possible for me to make a bargain with my neighbour to stop mowing the lawn and make both of us better off. If this transaction were to take place, the externality is said to be *internalized*.

Solving the world's environmental problems is obviously a lot more complicated than paying a neighbour to stop mowing the lawn on a Sunday morning. In the case of global warming, literally billions of people contribute to the release of greenhouse gases. Most of us only consider the private cost of our actions - like barbecuing sausages or driving to work - and not the social cost that these actions (burning of propane with a gas barbecue or the exhaust from a car) impose on others in terms of increased greenhouse gases in the atmosphere. This externality or divergence between private and social cost

18

leads to an inappropriate amount of consumption or production of goods and resources.

Given that many activities cause externalities, it is neither possible nor even desirable to prohibit every action that results in an externality. Instead, the goal should be to balance the benefits we receive from consumption and production with the costs that might be imposed on the rest of society. For example, we should compare the benefits associated with reading books with their environmental costs. The extra benefit society receives from books should be just equal to the extra cost they impose on society. This cost is in two parts: a private cost incurred by the authors, publisher and book retailers, and an external cost from the loss to society from a reduction in the number of mature trees. The private cost and the external cost together equal the social cost of producing the book. If the extra or *marginal social benefit* exceeds the extra or *marginal social cost* of books we should print more books and if the marginal social benefit is less than the marginal social cost we should print fewer books.

The desirable amount of a good - where its marginal social benefit equals the marginal social cost - is illustrated graphically in Figure 2.1. The vertical axis measures the benefits and costs of an activity in dollars and cents (or pounds and pence) while the horizontal axis measures the quantity produced or consumed of a good. In the figure are drawn three curves or lines that represent the marginal social benefit (MSB) of consuming the good and the marginal social cost (MSC) and marginal private cost (MPC) of producing the good. The marginal social benefit slopes down to the right because the higher the price of a good the fewer people we would expect to be both willing and able to pay for it. For example, very few people may value a can of cola at $10.00/can but a lot of people may value it at $0.50/can. The marginal private cost slopes up to the right indicating that, in general, the cost of producing an extra unit of a good increases with the number produced. The marginal social cost is the sum of the marginal private cost and the marginal external cost - the cost imposed on the rest of society by producing an extra can of cola. For instance, these external costs could come from the improper disposal of empty cola cans or direct damage to the environment from cola production itself because of, say, water pollution.

If a cola factory were left alone, it would continue to produce cola until the return to its owners from selling an extra can of cola exactly equalled the cost of producing it. If the return from the last can is greater than its cost, the factory could increase profits by increasing output. Similarly, if the return from the last can of cola is less than its cost of production, the factory is better off reducing output. The marginal social benefit of cola is reflected by its price.

Thus, where the marginal social benefit curve in Figure 2.1 equals the marginal private cost of the factory at Q' we find the desirable output from the viewpoint of the firm. This output is *not* the desirable output from the perspective of society because the cola factory imposes an external cost (such as improperly disposed of cans) on others which it does not consider. The desirable social output is at Q* where the marginal social benefit equals the marginal social cost.

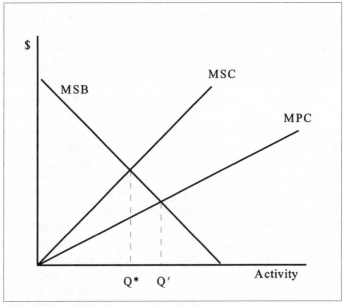

Figure 2.1   Desirable level of an activity

That the firm wants to produce more than the socially desirable amount should not be surprising. It arises because the firm does not face all the costs of its actions.

The fact that the production of cola imposes a cost on the rest of society does *not* mean that cola should be banned. It does mean, however, that its external cost should be taken into consideration when determining the appropriate level of output. For example, it is accepted by many that increased emissions of greenhouse gases, such as carbon dioxide and methane, increase the likelihood of global warming. Although global warming could have a disastrous impact on some people, this does not imply that all human-made greenhouse gas emissions should be prohibited. Apart from the fact that this is technically infeasible, it is also very undesirable. Some have estimated, for instance, that just to *stabilize* world greenhouse gas emissions at their 1990 level would cost about 4 per cent of the total world output (Weyant, 1993), an amount greater than the total annual income (excluding China and India) of the world's poorest 100 countries. To ban all emissions would cost immeasurably more, as illustrated in Figure 2.2. The total costs associated with different reductions in greenhouse gas emissions are not just numbers in bank accounts but represent real resources and assets which cannot be used for building hospitals and schools, providing clean drinking water, and a host of other essential services. We do not mean to suggest that a reduction or stabilization of greenhouse emissions is not desirable for many countries, particularly those found in the tropics, only that the costs must be balanced against the expected benefits.

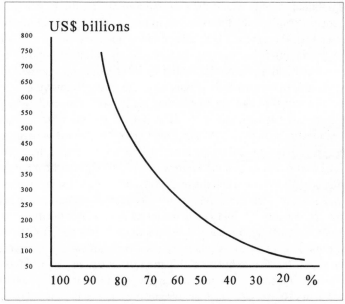

Figure 2.2 Costs associated with reductions in CO_2 baseline emissions. Source: Nordhaus, 1991.

An Appropriate Level of Pollution

Our cola example assumed that the external cost from the production of cola was fixed. In reality, the relationship between the consumption and production of a good and the external cost it imposes on society evolves over time due to improvements in technology or changes in the environment. The policies society imposes on individuals and firms also affect this relationship. Nevertheless, the desirable outcome from the point of view of society is always to ensure that the marginal social benefit of a good or action equals its marginal social cost. Instead of talking about the desirable or appropriate amount of a good, however, we could also discuss the appropriate level of pollution. The concept of an "appropriate" level of pollution may seem strange at first because pollution, by definition, is undesirable. What we mean is that just as pollution imposes costs on society so too does the control and reduction of pollution. Society's goal should be to equate these costs such that the cost of reducing a unit of pollution exactly equals the cost imposed by an extra unit of pollution. If we reduce pollution until the extra cost of removing another unit of emissions is greater than the external cost this emission imposes on society, we then become better off if we transfer resources from pollution control to other activities like building hospitals. Similarly, if the extra cost imposed from an additional unit of emissions is greater than the cost of removing it, society would be better off by putting more resources into reducing pollution.

The trade-off between the costs of pollution and the costs of reducing pollution may be depicted graphically as in Figure 2.3. On the vertical axis we measure costs in dollars and on the horizontal axis we measure the quantity of emissions or discharges. In the figure we have two curves, the marginal cost of abatement (MCA) curve and the marginal external cost (MEC) curve. The marginal cost of abatement represents the cost of reducing the level of emissions by one unit. It slopes up to the left to indicate that the more we clean up the more it costs us to reduce an extra unit of emissions. For example, to reduce emissions in cars it is relatively easy to install catalytic converters to exhaust pipes, but the complete elimination of emissions would involve the replacement of the internal combustion engine by a more expensive alternative. The marginal external cost curve represents the extra cost imposed on society by a small increase in the level of emissions. It slopes up to the right to indicate that an increase in emissions imposes a greater cost on society when emissions are high than when they are low. For example, a small increase in car emissions in an uncongested city may impose only a small cost on society. The same increase when car emissions are high could be the difference between living and dying for people with chronic lung complaints. The acceptable level of pollution is e* where the marginal cost of abatement equals the marginal external cost. If emissions exceed e*, the cost of reducing an extra unit of emissions is less than the external cost imposed by the extra unit, so we need to reduce emissions. Similarly, if emissions are less than e* we have reduced emissions too much because the extra cost from reducing emissions is greater than the cost it imposes on society.

While the above analysis has society accepting a positive amount of pollution, in some cases it is possible that the marginal external cost exceeds the

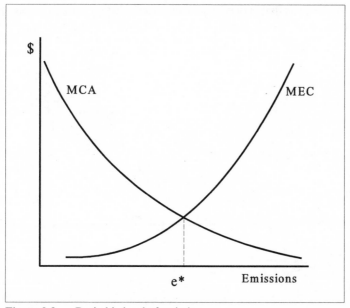

Figure 2.3   Desirable level of emissions

marginal cost of abatement at *all* level of emissions. In this situation, the desirable level of emissions equates to a zero level of pollution. This situation is illustrated in Figure 2.4. A zero level of emissions may be desirable if the pollutant imposes a very high cost on society and/or alternative methods of production are available that do not generate the pollutant. For example, the pesticide DDT was banned in many countries in the late 1960s and early 1970s after it was discovered to be accumulating in the food chain and having a negative affect on a number of wildlife species, especially birds. At the time, other chemicals and alternative farming practices were readily available to replace it.

On a global scale, the discharge of chemicals such as halons and chlorofluorocarbons (CFCs) into the atmosphere damages the ozone layer. Although the potential consequences of using these gases have been known since 1973, it was only after the discovery of a large ozone hole over Antarctica in 1985 that the problem was taken seriously. The ozone layer permits much of the life on earth by shielding it from the sun's ultraviolet radiation. Ozone-destroying chemicals, although widely used, represent only a tiny fraction of total economic activity and can be replaced by other chemicals. In contrast, the costs that ozone-destroying chemicals may impose on our planet are considerable. For instance, Australia and New Zealand, which are closest

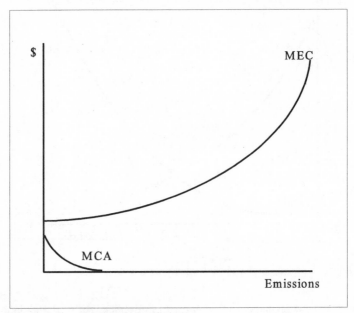

Figure 2.4   Zero level of emission

to the southern ozone hole, have the highest rates of skin cancer in the world. The concern is such that schoolchildren are advised to avoid being outside between 10:00 a.m and 2:00 p.m and are told to "slip on a shirt, slap on a hat and slop on sunblock". In addition to increasing rates of skin cancer, a thinning of the ozone layer reduces our immune response to other diseases, and increases the chance of blindness and other ailments.

Given the costs and benefits of banning CFCs, most people would agree that a zero level of pollution is desirable. Indeed, the prohibition of the production and trade of these chemicals through international agreements, such as the Montreal Protocol, is one of the environmental successes of the past decade.

Finding an Optimum

A fundamental question posed when determining an appropriate level of pollution is exactly how do we measure external costs? In the case of global warming, we can only predict likely scenarios given different levels of greenhouse gas emissions. We do not know what will happen and in fact a few scientists do not even believe that it will actually happen. Once the climate predictions are made, we then need to estimate the social and economic effects of global warming. These include estimates of its affect on flooding, changes in regional climates that could lead to monsoon failures and droughts, and the attendant consequences for livestock and crop production.

Trying to determine the impact of global warming not only illustrates the problem of *uncertainty* in estimating the costs and benefits of controlling pollution, but also the importance of taking into account *intergenerational equity*. For example, while controlling the emissions of greenhouse gases places a greater burden on the current generation than it does on future ones, the benefits of preventing or slowing down the rate of global warming will be enjoyed relatively more by future generations. How can these intergenerational costs and benefits be compared? One method for comparing costs and benefits over time is to discount the future to reflect the fact that a $1.00 benefit today is worth more than a $1.00 benefit ten years hence. One problem with discounting is that *any* costs incurred in the present can easily exceed discounted benefits in the distant future. Taking it to the extreme, when decisions are only based upon the discounted benefits less costs criterion, it is possible to justify decisions that would lead to the virtual extinction of future generations provided that such decisions generated higher discounted net benefits! (Page, 1977, pp. 243-251).

Determining a desirable level of pollution should also take account of so-called *threshold effects*. These arise whenever the cost of pollution rapidly increases after a given point or threshold. For example, with global warming most countries can adapt without too much difficulty to a 1-1.5°C increase in the average world temperature. Unfortunately, past a certain temperature threshold there may be enormous increases in costs. For instance, if temperatures were to rise so that the Antarctic ice cap melted, the sea-level would rise 55 metres - an amount sufficient to completely flood many of the world's major cities including Shanghai, Tokyo, London and New York, and submerge entire countries and most of the world's river deltas where hundreds of millions of people live.

In calculating the appropriate level of pollution we also have to consider *irreversibilities* which may prevent us from reaching a desired outcome. In the case of global warming, even if we were to reduce greenhouse gas emissions our past discharges may have moved us into a completely different climate such that we can never return to where we would have been in the absence of these discharges. The most dramatic example of an irreversibility is the extinction of a species. Barring a Jurassic Park scenario, a species that is lost is gone forever.

So far we have explained the notion of an externality and what is an appropriate level of pollution. We have also considered the difficulties in calculating this optimal outcome. In reality, society does the best it can to determine some acceptable level of pollution and then tries to arrive at this outcome. Let's look now at the various classes of pollution with which society has to grapple.

2.2   TYPES OF POLLUTION

When experts characterize the types of pollution, they usually have in mind a number of questions. Is the polluting source mobile or stationary? Does the pollutant come from one well-defined (point) source or various sources (non-point)? Does the pollutant accumulate or disperse? And, are the effects of the pollution local, national or global?

Mobile versus Stationary Polluters

To classify pollution as mobile simply means that the polluting source itself has the ability to move about. By far the most common source of *mobile* pollution are automobiles.

Example 2.1: Automobile Emissions and Smog in Mexico City

At least one half of the air pollution in Mexico City results from the emissions of automobiles, trucks and buses. This city boasts about 2.5 million motor vehicles which, in 1989, burned about 1 million barrels of leaded petroleum each day. Most of the vehicular traffic takes place during peak rush hours, leading to particularly high concentrations of emissions at these times.

On average, only about 20 days a year in Mexico city are considered to have "satisfactory" air. Residents experience sore eyes, noses and throats. Respiratory problems abound in the children and elderly of the city. Cancer, such as leukaemia in children, has also been linked to air pollution. Automobile emissions have resulted in lead poisoning, with young children being particularly susceptible. If exposed at an early age, lead can result in lower IQ and neurobehavioural problems.

Gasoline-powered automobiles emit a variety of pollutants into the air. The most prevalent are carbon dioxide, carbon monoxide, nitrogen oxides, hydrocarbons and, whenever leaded gasoline is used, lead. Part of the difficulty with controlling automobile emissions is that there are literally millions of vehicles on the road, each of which contributes a minute quantity to the total emissions. No driver, therefore, has the incentive to reduce his or her emissions as any individual driver's reduction in fuel consumption has a tiny impact on the total problem.

Each automobile constitutes a well-defined emissions source. However, because one cannot determine precisely if it were a particular automobile that emitted any given substance, automobile emissions may be best considered as constituting a *non-point* polluting source. Furthermore, these emissions typically do not accumulate, i.e., they are *non-stock* pollutants. The impact of automobile emissions tends to be *local* insofar as air quality is concerned. However, since this is a *mobile* polluting source, an automobile's emissions can clearly affect a number of jurisdictions. In addition, once these emissions have been exhausted into the air, wind may cause these pollutants to cross borders, rendering the impact of the pollutant *national* or even *international* in effect.

Source: UNEP (1992); Eskeland (1992).

Point versus Non-Point Sources

When environmentalists talk about point and non-point sources, they are referring to whether the source of the pollution is clearly identifiable. For instance, a pulp and paper mill discharging chlorinated water into a stream is a *point* source since it is a well-defined source of the pollutant. However, the run-off of pesticides, herbicides and fertilizers from farm land is a non-point source of pollution because it is often impossible to properly identify the precise site or source of the pollutants.

Let's look at some more examples to show what we mean by point and non-point sources of pollution.

Example 2.2: Three Mile Island Nuclear Facility, Pennsylvania, U.S.

Until the April 1986 Chernobyl accident, the Three Mile Island nuclear reactor in the U.S. held the dubious distinction of being the world's worst civil nuclear disaster. It was caused mainly by human error. The accident occurred when a mechanical failure shut down the reactor. Water pumps were then triggered to cool the reactor and a relief valve opened to let the water and steam go into the reactor's containment vessel. However, this valve was left open for too long and the reactor began to overheat as the water meant to cool it escaped through the faulty relief valve. The emergency cooling system was mistakenly shut off; with the reactor's core reaching almost 3,000 degrees Celsius (some 5000 degrees Fahrenheit). The top part of the core melted and, when water was finally released into the reactor, the remainder of the core shattered from the shock of the cool water. Thus low levels of radiation were released into the atmosphere.

Upwards of 200,000 people living within a fifty-mile radius of the nuclear facility fled from the area in an attempt to reduce their exposure to radiation. Pregnant women and children were evacuated. The release of low-level radiation is also blamed for the above-average death rates of the elderly in the area surrounding the plant although this may be caused by other factors, such as high levels of naturally occurring radiation from radon in the area near Three Mile Island. The Three Mile Island reactor is a point source of pollution. The radiation emerging from this power plant in 1979 came from a well-defined source. The source is also stationary. Radiation is a particularly interesting pollutant since, although it would technically disappear once the polluting source stopped emitting it, radiated substances have extremely long half lives, suggesting that one should best think of radiated material as constituting stock pollutants. The effects of this type of pollution are local, national and international. In the case of the Three Mile Island event, the effects were contained primarily within the area surrounding the plant, since it was a low-level radiation leak. Chernobyl, by contrast, affected virtually the entire continent of Europe.

Sources: Rees (1985); Meshkati (1991).

Point sources, therefore, are clearly identifiable as the emitters of a given substance. Knowing from where a pollutant is emitted makes the task of the regulator much easier. However, as the Lake Dillon Reservoir in Colorado example illustrates, while point source pollutants are the most straightforward to identify and regulate, policy makers have made innovative inroads towards control of non-point sources as well.

Example 2.3: Lake Dillon Reservoir, Colorado, U.S.

The Lake Dillon Reservoir was created in 1963 and provides an important source of water and recreational activities for north-central Colorado. Water quality deteriorated considerably over the decade of the 1970s, likely due to the rapid changes in land uses during this time. The main problem with the water was the presence of phosphates.

Almost 80 per cent of the phosphates come from *non-point* sources. About 50 per cent of the phosphates come from run-offs and erosion from nearby construction sites as well as direct precipitation on the lake from so-called "natural" sources. The remaining pollution stems from human-induced non-point sources like septic systems. These contributors constitute non-point sources since it is impossible to determine precisely from which source these pollutants emanate. Run-offs, for instance, occur at numerable locations around the lake. The remaining phosphates in the lake are from well-defined *point* sources like water treatment plants.

Government intervention is geared towards correcting the misuse of this resource by creating private property rights for effluent discharges. In particular, tradeable rights for phosphorus have been established. One of the unique attributes of this transferable right scheme is that any growth in point source pollution is to be accommodated only by non-point source reductions.   In other words, effluent trading is encouraged between point and non-point sources. Various problems arise from polluting this reservoir. Water contamination has health consequences, particularly among those with weaker immune systems, like the very young or old. Individuals' livelihoods are threatened because of its impact on, for instance, the recreational fishery, as well as the resulting loss of revenue associated with tourism.

Sources: Northwest Colorado Council of Governments (1984); Hahn and Hester (1989).

The situation in the Lake Dillon Reservoir is rather unique. Point sources, in order to increase emissions beyond their regulated level, had to identify and acquire rights from non-point sources. This set-up has a number of appealing features: it overcomes one of the biggest problems associated with the regulation of non-point source emissions - their identification. Point sources into Lake Dillon were induced to seek out and find non-point ones. Similarly, non-point sources that were willing to reduce their emissions - for compensation of course - were given the incentive to be "found". For such a system to work the geographic scope of the scheme has to be quite small. Well-defined bodies of water are ideal in this regard. In many ways, it is surprising that more examples do not exist of schemes which encourage trade between point and non-point sources.

Stock Pollutants

Many pollutants do not accumulate over time. While their effects may be cumulative - as, for instance the effect of increasing levels of carbon monoxide in Mexico City - they do not always physically accumulate as they continue to be emitted. For these substances, society is concerned with the strength of their flow.   Some pollutants do however accumulate, leading to a different environmental problem. How should society dispose of these accumulating hazardous wastes? This problem is not merely one of finding a site for their storage. The disposing of hazardous wastes encompasses a whole host of difficulties.

Example 2.4: Disposing of Nuclear Waste

A substantial quantity of nuclear wastes is generated annually worldwide. Aside from the enormous difficulties associated with finding dumps to physically accommodate this waste, the problem is further complicated by the fact that this waste exudes radioactivity that persists for very long periods of time. Plutonium, for instance, which is a byproduct of nuclear fission and can be used to fuel nuclear reactors, has a half life of about 25,000 years.

Some 425 nuclear reactors operate worldwide. A typical reactor generates about 30 tons of so-called commercial "spent" fuel (i.e., the uranium, plutonium, and other elements that fuel the reactors) per year. In the United States alone, about 50,000 metric tons of this commercial spent fuel and other wastes will have accumulated by the year 2000.

This commercial spent fuel, however, is but one of a host of nuclear wastes generated annually. Other wastes include the liquid wastes from nuclear generation, and spent wastes from nuclear research and weapons' production. For instance, the former Soviet Union's and the United States' dismantling of nuclear warheads will result in almost 300 tons of unneeded plutonium and almost 1,000 tons of uranium. In addition to these "high-level" wastes - referring to their extreme radioactivity - a much larger quantity of low-level wastes is also generated.

At the moment, in the United States much of this waste is housed in temporary facilities. Imagine the problems associated with finding a permanent storage site? To get an idea of the enormity of the problem of nuclear waste disposal, consider the following example. In Canada, the agency that was set up to support and regulate the nuclear industry, the Atomic Energy of Canada Limited, after some 15 years of research into the problem recently came up with a proposal of how to dispose of nuclear wastes permanently in the rock bed known as the Canadian Shield. The federal government is holding public hearings into the matter. According to the Atomic Energy of Canada Limited it will take another 20 years of research and about 400 jobs merely to *choose* the appropriate site. Once it is chosen, the construction of the site will take another five to seven years. The actual running of the site would employ about 1,000 people annually and would operate for between 50 and 60 years.

Sources: Fass (1988); Morrison (1992); www.ontarionorth.com/ feb96/nuclear.htm; Hahn (1988).

The problems associated with stock pollutants are formidable. It is especially troublesome to learn of the catastrophic consequences stemming from the mishandling of toxic wastes - which are clearly shown by the now infamous Love Canal fiasco. Love Canal was a small community in upstate New York, located near Niagara Falls. From 1942 to 1952 a large chemical company (Hooker Chemicals) buried its wastes in an abandoned waterway known as Love Canal. It then virtually gave the land to a local board of education upon which an elementary school was built. A residential community sprung up around the area. This community became famous in 1978 when residents began complaining about chemicals seeping to the surface, causing a variety of strange incidents. Love Canal was declared a disaster area and abandoned as a residential neighbourhood shortly thereafter, once the magnitude of health problems stemming from the oozing toxicity was discovered. One result of Love Canal was the establishment of stringent legislation forcing all contributors to a hazardous waste dump to be liable for any damages arising from the dump (the *Comprehensive Environmental Response, Compensation and Liability Act* of 1980). Clearly, pollutants that stockpile pose special difficulties for governments (Callan and Thomas, 1996, pp.539-540; Carter, 1987).

Local, national and global pollutants

The impact of particular pollutants may be local, national and/or global. Substances, like carbon dioxide, lead to national and even global effects via their impact on, say, global warming. Other pollutants, like lead have much clearer local effects. Let's look now at a couple of extreme examples of pollutants and the geographic extent of their effects.

Example 2.5: The Aral Sea

The Aral Sea, located inland about 2,500 kilometres south of Moscow, bordering the former soviet republics of Kazakhstan and Uzbekistan, is held up to be one of the worst human-made ecological disasters of the modern world. Although its impact is essentially local in nature, the lessons derived from this experience have shocked the world and are regarded as an example of the disastrous consequences of tampering with nature.

During the 1960s, officials in Moscow decided to try to expand the production of cotton in the region surrounding the Aral Sea. Cotton was considered to be "white gold" for the region; a one-crop policy was thus actively pursued. To do this, the rivers feeding the sea were diverted by massive irrigation projects, resulting in the sea's water falling some 47 feet, more than 25 per cent of its total depth. The volume of the sea diminished by two thirds, with its area shrinking by almost one half.

The area surrounding the Aral Sea was worst hit. The rivers feeding the sea were considerably diminished and heavily laden with the polluted run-off from pesticide-infested farm lands. The health consequences of this alone were staggering. The moderating influence of the sea on the climate of the region also changed. Increased snowfall affected the region's cotton plants; and the ensuing hot, dry summers contributed to the desertification of the region. Salinization increased tremendously in the sea itself, which led to salt being spread in dust storms to hitherto fertile grounds with predictable results.

Fishing villages found themselves miles from water, with no way for their inhabitants to eke out a reasonable living. Those working in the cotton fields were exposed to pesticides, leading to irreversible health effects. And, as land continued to diminish in productivity, the few fertile areas in which other agricultural crops were raised were pressed into cotton production. In effect, the economy of the entire region became dependent on cotton production, which, as its yield diminished, left hundreds of thousands of people destitute.

While the area immediately around the sea was hit the hardest, communities all along the contributory rivers were affected by their heavily polluted waters. For instance, bacterial levels in the drinking water of the region of Ptosis, about 200 kilometres south of the Aral Sea, were over ten times greater than the permitted standard. Many individuals in this region became sick, and it recorded the highest infant mortality rate in the entire Soviet Union.

Source: Feshbach and Friendly (1992, chapter 4).

As the Aral Sea example so aptly illustrates, the fact that a pollutant or some sort of environmental degradation is local in nature does not imply that its effects are not devastating. That we even know about the travesty surrounding the Aral Sea is a testament to how strong its impact was and continues to be. While the Aral Sea disaster may be classified as local or national in nature, other problems are much more international in scope. The destruction of the ozone layer surely epitomizes an international environmental problem. Because no one is immune to the potential implications of the thinning of stratospheric ozone, international cooperation is essential to combat the causes of this problem.

Example 2.6: Ozone Layer Destruction

At the edge of our atmosphere lies the stratospheric ozone layers which protects our planet from the sun's ultraviolet (UV) radiation. Recent evident suggests that some synthetic compounds, most notably halons and chlorofluorocarbons (CFCs), are contributing to the thinning of this layer thus increasing the amount of harmful UV radiation reaching the earth's surface. Increased exposure to UV rays is shown to increase the incidence of skin cancer. And, by damaging the skin, an individual's natural defences are weakened, potentially leading to the contraction of infectious diseases. It also causes eye problems like cataracts and photo keratitis (snowblindness).

The release of chlorine in the CFCs depletes the ozone layer. CFCs are used primarily as coolants in refrigeration systems. They have also been used as propellants in aerosol cans and in a few other applications. Halons are chemically stable compounds that have been widely used in fire extinguishers. They contain the compound "bromine" which is ten-times more powerful in terms of ozone depletion when compared to the chlorine in CFCs. However, they are used much less often than are CFCs.

The destruction of the ozone layer is of global significance. While certain areas of the world may be affected more dramatically than others, like in Antarctica, Australia, New Zealand, Chile, Argentina and South Africa, all inhabitants of the world are potentially harmed by the increased UV rays.

On 22 March 1985 delegates from around the world attended the Vienna Convention for the Protection of the Ozone Layer (the Vienna convention). From this meeting, a group was established to develop a protocol for the use of ozone-harming substances. This protocol was adopted in Montreal on 16 September 1987. By 1993, 100 countries plus the European Union, accounting for over 95 per cent of worldwide consumption of these substances, had signed the agreement.

The Montreal protocol resulted in the adoption of a schedule for the reduction in the use of CFCs and halons. The use of CFCs is to be totally eliminated by the year 2000, while their production and export are already prohibited. The 1992 Copenhagen revisions to this protocol dictate the elimination of halons by the year 2010.

Sources: Benedick (1991); Parson (1993); *Environsense* at http://es.inel.gov/program/epaorgs/oar/epa-oar1.html.

2.3   EXTERNALITIES, ECONOMICS AND THE ENVIRONMENT

The economics approach to environmental problems focuses on the importance of identifying externalities when trying to determine an effective policy. Rather than condoning problems like pollution, the economics framework highlights the need to determine all of the costs and benefits associated with activities in order to ascertain whether or not a particular activity should continue. For instance, almost no one would argue that we should do without motor vehicles even though they constitute a source of pollution. However, almost everyone would agree that policies should "encourage" automobile manufacturers to produce cleaner cars. Similarly, that carbon-fuels are typically subject to some kind of tax seems reasonable as a way to induce drivers to limit the number of kilometres driven. Thus, the notion of an "appropriate" amount of pollution is intimately tied to the benefits as well as the costs associated with productive activities. The easier (cheaper) it is to abate pollution, the less pollution society will decide to accept. Of course, some circumstances warrant the total elimination of pollutants - when it is clear that they impose tremendous costs on society or when too much uncertainty exists as to their potential costs, and so on.

The type of pollutant also affects the way in which policy makers can influence its production. Mobile pollutants may require different measures than do stationary ones. Pollutants that are local in impact may be dealt with quite differently than would pollutants that migrate across international borders.

Substances which stockpile rather than dissipate also pose special problems. In short, knowing the characteristics of the pollution problem provides us with useful information that can be used to help "solve" the problem, as the various examples of this chapter so aptly illustrate.

2.4   FURTHER READING

Some very accessible books on externalities and the environment are Dales (1968), Field and Olewiler (1995), Callan and Thomas (1996), Hodge (1995a), Seneca and Taussig (1984), Turner *et al.* (1994) and Tietenberg (1994). We also recommend chapters 2 and 3 of Baumol and Oates (1988) which provide an excellent discussion of externalities.

A basic introduction to the problems of global warming is provided by Neal (1989) while Schelling (1993) provides a very interesting view of the economics of global warming. Tietenberg (1994, pp. 262-271) and Callan and Thomas (1996, chapter 12) also provide nice reviews of the problems of global warming and depletion of atmospheric ozone. A very detailed study on global warming is Cline (1992a). Somerville (1996) is a particularly good reference on the effects of air pollution on the atmosphere. Optimistic perspectives on global warming are presented in Balling (1995) and Michaels (1995) while Flavin (1996) emphasizes the dangers. A nice overview of climate change is found chapter 2 of Pickering and Owen (1994). A detailed economic treatment of the economic impacts of global warming is given in Dornbusch and Poterba (1991) and Nordhaus (1993) while Cline (1992b) provides estimates of the benefits of abatement. An up-to-date and detailed review of the economic and social impacts of global warming is provided by Bruce *et al.* (1996) while Paterson (1996) and Mabey *et al.* (1997) provide nice descriptions and analyses of the political economy of global warming. If you want more information on the causes and consequences of depletion of the ozone layer we recommend, Parson (1993) and chapter 3 of Pickering and Owen (1994).

Hahn and Hester (1989) provide a very clear discussion of the theory of tradeable permits, as well as a nice review of some examples. A good description of the problems of air pollution in large cities is provided by the United Nations Environment Programme (1992). The many problems associated with nuclear waste are discussed at some length in Carter (1987). For a detailed discussion of the environmental situation in the former Soviet Union we recommend Feshbach and Friendly (1992) and Bridges and Bridges (1996).

3

Property Rights for Pollution

3.1   THE PROBLEM

In any given day in Mexico City, breathing air can be dangerous. The 21 million or so individuals of the world's largest city cannot take for granted that this necessity of life will not make them sick. In North America and elsewhere, people listen for the forecasted ultraviolet radiation index before deciding on their daily activities because spending even a few hours in the summer sun can be a health hazard.

How can it be that participating in activities as natural as breathing and strolling in the park are now considered by some to be life threatening? Although the reasons for dirty air in Mexico City are different from those that have increased UV exposure, the basic cause of these two problems is the same - pollution. Pollution does not only result in problems of a grand scale, but it affects us daily in numerous ways. Neighbours playing music too loudly affect our ability to enjoy peace and quiet. Garbage strewn in the park lessens our enjoyment of the outdoors. Proximity to magnetic fields can increase the likelihood of cancer. And the list goes on.

From our examples in Chapter 2, we know that an across-the-board policy of zero pollution is often not in society's best interest. One way to "solve" the pollution problem is to establish private property rights for pollution. Here, we show how this solution works by focusing on real-world cases where property rights have been used. As you will see, while property rights cannot solve all pollution problems, in the right circumstances they go a long way in correcting them. Before turning to these cases, we need to detail exactly what we mean by property rights.

3.2   PROPERTY RIGHTS

An important way to make people consider the external costs they impose on others is to create property rights or modify existing, inadequate ones. Property rights affect our lives in many ways. If we own a car or motorbike our right to this property is certified in ownership papers; anyone using our vehicle without permission faces the risk of prosecution and even imprisonment. A property right can also be owned by a community, as is the case with common grazing land that exists in many parts of the world. Property rights may also be owned by a society as a whole as with national parks or by no one at all, as with fish in the high seas.

Property rights are defined in terms of owner(s) and their relationship with others regarding the asset. A property right provides a stream of benefits to the owner (or user) and requires that others respect the property right (Bromley, 1991). Who owns the property right and how this right is specified affects its use. For example, we may drive a car differently if we own it than if we rent it. Similarly, how property rights - the rights people have to use goods and resources - are specified in terms of the environment and natural resources can be the difference between having a desirable world to live in or one where resources are over exploited and people have a poor quality of life.

Characteristics of Property Rights

Comparing property rights for different goods and resources is difficult because property rights have many characteristics. Simply saying that something is privately or communally owned is not sufficient to describe a property right. For example, in traditional Polynesian communities goods that are privately owned can be "borrowed" (if there is a need) without prior agreement by fellow members of the community. This form of private ownership is less *exclusive* than what exists in the western world. In most countries, land can be transferred through purchase or inheritance. In some places like the Cook Islands in the South Pacific, however, foreigners are not permitted to own land while in other countries no restrictions are placed on the *transferability* of residential property. Property rights can also be described in terms of *divisibility*. Land ownership could, for instance, be split among different owners into surface rights for building and farming or other uses and sub-surface rights or mineral rights. Another characteristic is the *quality of title* of the property right. In several developing countries, farmers may not have proper title or deed to land upon which they are farming, preventing them from using the property as collateral for loans. One other important characteristic is the *duration* of the property right. In some countries with a British tradition of property rights, land can be "owned" in 99 year leases or as freehold with no fixed term of ownership. Finally, *flexibility* refers to how the property right can accommodate changes in both the asset and the circumstances of the owner. For example, in times past in northern Europe the tradition, and indeed obligation, was that land passed on from one generation to the next had to go to the eldest son. Such a rule was inflexible (and discriminatory!) to the circumstances of the owner. In the early years of American history land was given free to settlers by the U.S. government provided it was cleared and/or developed in some way. In this case, inflexibility was deliberately introduced into the property right so as to encourage settlement and discourage land speculation. Overlaying all the characteristics is *enforceability* of the property right by the owner(s).

Figure 3.1 illustrates these six characteristics of property rights. The arrows represent the *dimension* of the property right, and do not imply interactions between the characteristics. When the arrow goes all the way to a characteristic, say exclusivity, this implies that the asset in question, for example a private motor vehicle, is exclusive. In contrast, the arrow to the divisibility characteristic in Figure 3.1 is not fully extended to the boundary of the circle indicating that the asset - a motor car - cannot be physically divided. Despite the fact that the dimension of the characteristics is a subjective measure, the framework can be readily applied to all types of property rights. Understanding the characteristics of these rights and how they can be changed represents an important step in helping to determine appropriate policies for improving our environment.

Many types of property rights exist, each with their own set of characteristics. Often property rights that have a similar set of characteristics are called *property-rights regimes*. The nature of these regimes is determined by the institutional setting, technology, and the aspect of the environment over which they are held. For example, land previously owned communally by indigenous populations became privately-owned following colonization by European settlers in such places as the United States, Australia, New Zealand and South Africa. This change in the property-right regime reflected differences in culture and institutions as well as different technologies and uses for the land.

Characteristics of Goods and Resources

Another crucial aspect of property rights is the characteristics of the good or resource over which the right it is held. Most of the world's environmental problems arise when the use of a good by someone affects how it can be used by someone else. In technical terms, a good is said to be *rivalrous* if its use by one person prevents someone else from using it. A car is a rivalrous good whereas breathing clean air may not be. Goods or resources may also be classified as *depletable* or *subtractable* whereby their use by someone reduces the amount available to others. They may also be described as *non-exclusive* such that others cannot be prevented from using the good or resource.

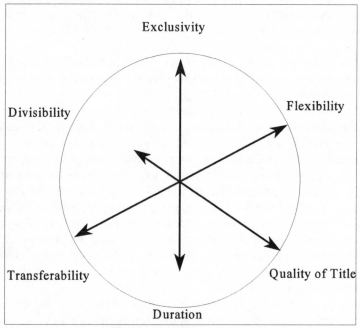

Figure 3.1   Characteristics of property rights

When a resource is rivalrous and non-exclusive it is called a *common-pool resource* and examples include the fish in the sea and many of the amenities we enjoy in the environment. Sometimes a natural resource or the environment is *congestible* rather than rivalrous. That is to say, our use has a negative impact on others only when there are a large number of users such as when we go hiking in the wilderness or whale watching.

A special type of good or resource which is neither rivalrous or congestible and is non-exclusive is called a *public good*. An example of a public good is a lighthouse - whether one or many people rely on it to help navigate does not affect the value of the lighthouse to each skipper who uses it. Further, once a lighthouse is in operation it can be used by anybody who can see the light (a "positive" externality). A type of good or resource which is congestible and where exclusion is relatively easy is called a *club good*. Examples of club goods are libraries or health clubs where users can easily be excluded; however, once membership reaches a certain number, extra members reduce the benefits to existing ones. Goods which are both rivalrous and exclusive are called *private goods*. For instance, a motor vehicle is a private good because its use is rivalrous (two people cannot drive the car at the same time) and exclusive (other people cannot use the car without a key or breaking the law).

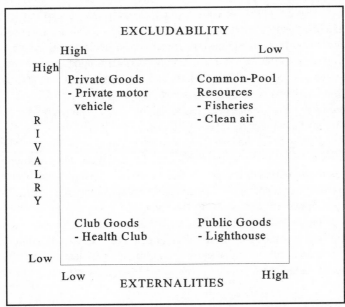

Figure 3.2   Characteristics of goods and resources

Different types of goods or resources are illustrated in Figure 3.2. The special nature of common-pool resources where exclusion is difficult, use is rivalrous and where the externalities imposed on others can be quite large, explains why such resources are often not managed in a desirable way.

Private Rights

Private property rights exist virtually everywhere - from our ownership of automobiles and houses to the clothes that we wear. However, the characteristics of the rights differ depending on the good or resource in question and the jurisdiction, institutions and culture in which they are applied. For instance, despite the widespread use of private property rights they have not often been used for common-pool resources. One explanation for this rests on the fact that to have a private property right of value we must be able to exclude - at least to some extent - others from using it. The inability to exclude makes it difficult to *alienate* common-pool resources such that the property right can be bought, sold or leased. For example, we would probably not bother buying a car if anyone could use it at any point in time. The ability to establish private property is also limited if our consumption, production or use of the property is affected by others. We may not pay as much money for an asset whose value is dependent on the production and consumption decisions of others as we would for an asset whose value was solely dependent upon our own actions. The less we are able to exclude others and the more our use is affected by others, the less likely we are to find private property rights.

Internalizing an externality by establishing private property rights may sometimes lead to what is called an *efficient* outcome. This outcome is efficient because society is doing the best it can with what it has. An efficient outcome, however, is not necessarily an *equitable* one. For example, when using private rights to control externalities in fisheries by initially giving all the harvesting rights to one fisher is not as "fair" as giving an equal amount to all fishers. Both allocations, however, can result in the same efficient outcome because the trading of harvesting rights can lead to fishers harvesting the same amount (after trading), irrespective of the initial allocation. This result, namely that private property rights (under certain conditions) will lead to an efficient outcome, is called the *Coase Theorem* after Ronald Coase, the 1991 Nobel

Laureate in Economics. The conditions that are required to ensure that the private property right outcome is efficient are:

▸ The *transaction costs* of exchanging private property rights are zero.

▸ People exchange their property rights without trying to manipulate the quantity and price at which they buy or sell to their own personal advantage.

▸ How much people own does not affect the value they place on an extra unit of the property right.

These conditions are almost never satisfied. Nevertheless, if transaction costs are relatively low and the markets for property rights are competitive, private property rights may lead to a better result than would other property-right regimes.

When deciding whether we should use private property rights to address a problem in the environment, we should neither reject them on the grounds that they "privatize" the environment nor accept them on the grounds that they will always lead to an efficient outcome. Rather, we should ask ourselves the following questions: is it possible to exclude persons from using the resource at a "reasonable" cost? If private property rights lead to changes in equity is it possible to compensate the "losers"? If private rights can lead to a net gain over alternative regimes they should be considered as a way of internalizing externalities.

3.3   PROPERTY RIGHTS AND POLLUTION

Creating a property right to pollute may result in the reduction of pollution to the socially acceptable level. One key feature that leads to this desirable result is that the rights are transferable. In other words, a "market" is established wherein trade may occur in the rights to pollute. To be effective, the right must be defined over some well-specified criterion: for instance, one right may give the owner permission to emit one unit of pollution. And, how the right is defined depends intimately upon the objectives of the policy maker.

Environmental policy may be geared towards two types of "targets". One target, called an *effluent standard*, expresses the goal of the policy in terms of a specific **quantity** of a given pollutant or pollutants. The current sulphur dioxide trading programme in the United States is an example of such a standard. The other target, called an *ambient standard*, is concerned with the **quality** of the environment in a well-specified area. Establishing a tradeable property rights scheme based on a quality-based standard is complicated. Among other things, it necessitates the determination of a well-defined quality standard that can be easily measured at regular intervals over time and space. One clear benefit of an ambient standard is the fact that it can regulate firms that emit more than one pollutant. Implementing an effluent standard on such firms is a complication and may be ineffective if firms are able to switch from emitting the "regulated" pollutant to a non-regulated one (Devlin & Grafton , 1994). However, setting permits based on an ambient standard for air pollution can be tricky because of wind patterns, transboundary polluters and so on. Ambient standards may be more easily employed for water pollution. The Fox River, Wisconsin, case detailed below provides an example of ambient-based permits.

Rather than discussing tradeable permits schemes "in theory" we think that it would be more interesting to look at a number of actual cases of tradeable property rights in action. You might be surprised to learn just how prevalent tradeable rights are in some jurisdictions. The United States, for instance, has relied on this type of environmental policy much more than any other country. As a result, four of the five cases presented in this chapter take place in the United States. However, tradeable property right schemes could easily be adopted elsewhere.

For the ease of exposition, it is useful to think of these schemes as targeting local, national or international environmental problems - while keeping in mind the fact that certain problems have elements of more than one characteristic. Three of the cases focus on a specific environmental target for the purposes of correcting a **local** problem: The RECLAIM programme of Southern California is geared towards cleaning the air in the Los Angeles Basin; the Bag Tag Programme in Gananoque, Canada, limits the amount of household refuse that may be disposed of in this town; and the Fox River Discharge Programme in the state of Wisconsin targets effluent discharges into the river. Another major programme in the United States - the sulphur dioxide trading programme - tries to correct the **national** problem of acid rain. Finally, our last case study looks at the U.S. trading programme for ozone-depleting substances which came about as a result of an international agreement limiting these substances.

Local Problems

One of the advantages of a local problem is that the major contributors are typically easy to identify. In addition, as long as powers are decentralized, the regulator may be relatively close to the problem and thus would be aware of any particular circumstances that may be influencing polluters' behaviour. We begin this subsection with a description of Southern California's RECLAIM programme, which is by far the most comprehensive tradeable permit scheme in existence to target a local pollution problem.

Case 3.1: The RECLAIM Programme of Southern California

The Problem

The Los Angeles Basin in Southern California has the dubious distinction of having the dirtiest air in the United States. It also has been grappling for decades with the problem of how to improve its air quality and meet U.S. Federal Environmental Protection Agency standards. The regulators entrusted to meet this objective in the South Coast Air Quality Management District (SCAQAM) have introduced a variety of schemes, with varying degrees of success. In an attempt to control the problem, the district implemented on 1 January 1994 a comprehensive and novel programme of tradeable emission credits called the Regional Clean Air Incentives Market (RECLAIM).

A Property Rights Solution

The RECLAIM policy is geared towards the larger emitters of ozone-depleting substances from stationary sources. Initially, emission trading can occur in two compounds - nitrogen oxides (NO_x) and sulphur dioxide (SO_x). All firms that emit four or more tons annually of these compounds are included in the programme. Some 391 firms began in the programme which has fallen slightly to 353 in 1996. Each facility is given an annual allocation of permits covering NO_x and SO_x,

---

based on past emissions. This amount is then ratcheted down each year - at different rates for each compound, reflecting federal environmental standards.

Firms have a number of options to be in compliance with the standards. They can use all of their allocated permits and reduce their emissions; they can choose to reduce emissions by employing more stringent abatement techniques freeing up some "emission reduction credits" (ERCs) which can be sold or saved for future use; or, firms may go to the market and buy some ERCs from other firms.

Over the past two years, trading in NO_X and SO_X has been fairly brisk. Participating firms have traded credits for more than 100,000 tons of these substances, at a market value of over \$10 million. Prices have ranged from an average of \$24 per ton for NO_X and \$13 per ton for SO_X for 1994 emissions, and considerably higher in the market for future emissions (for instance, \$1,529 for NO_X credits for the year 2009 and \$960 for SO_X credits in 1998).

Characteristics of the Property Right

In the RECLAIM programme firms have a property right over certain emissions. This right is fully *transferable*, although the market within which such trades are likely to occur is geographically quite limited. Furthermore, because firms in this programme differ quite substantially among each other, this may add to the cost of finding a suitable partner with which to trade. The right is measured in tons of emissions. The *quality of title* seems to be quite good. However, as with all assets arising from public policy, their quality and *duration* are subject to the vagaries of the political process. The tradeable credits established by the RECLAIM programme are designed to be rather flexible. They can be kept by their initial "owners" or sold to other firms. Figure 3.3 illustrates the characteristics of the property right created by RECLAIM's emission-reduction credit programme.

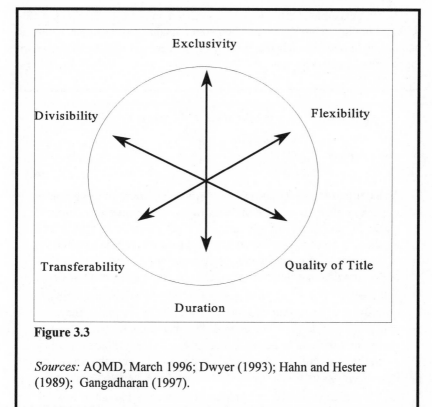

Figure 3.3

Sources: AQMD, March 1996; Dwyer (1993); Hahn and Hester (1989); Gangadharan (1997).

One of the interesting features of the RECLAIM programme is that it allows trading in more than one substance. This scheme is focused on cleaning the air in the Los Angeles Basin. The success of the programme is due, in large part, to the flexibility that is accorded the various point source emitters in this region. Rather than considering RECLAIM as an additional constraint on their behaviour, firms are encouraged to use the trade of emission-reduction credits to further their own objectives. For instance, firms may enter into this market as long as they purchase sufficient ERCs to support their emissions. Thus, even in the situation where the local air cannot safely sustain any more pollution, the economy remains dynamic.

The next example of a property rights scheme to control a local externality is found in the small town of Gananoque in Canada. This example, while not technically a tradeable scheme, provides further insight into the usefulness of the property rights approach.

Case 3.2: Solving the Household Waste Problem?

The Problem

As landfills are used up, and as land surrounding urban centres becomes more and more scarce, the problem of how to dispose of household waste becomes increasingly important. This issue is particularly sensitive in densely populated countries. However, even in a country as vast as Canada, municipalities are searching for new and creative ways of encouraging individuals to reduce, reuse and recycle their waste.

It may be surprising to learn that in North America individuals typically are not constrained as to the quantity of waste they can generate. Nor do they face charges that increase with the amount of waste they personally generate. As a result, many households pay virtually no attention to the types of products they buy, the packaging in which they come, or the waste generated from their consumption.

One way to encourage individuals to reduce the amount of garbage they create, is to limit the quantity of refuse that can be disposed of each period and/or to charge them for each waste container individuals fill. For instance, each household may have the right to throw away two bags of waste per week. This policy has the potential to reduce the amount of waste generated by households in comparison to the situation of no limits or no charges.

Some towns, faced with closing landfill sites and nowhere to put mounting garbage, are implementing schemes that are designed to encourage the reduction of waste. The town of Gananoque - a small tourist town on the banks of the St. Lawrence river some 250 kilometres from Toronto - provides one such example.

A Property-Rights Solution

With the closure of its only waste dumping site, the town of Gananoque was faced with a potentially substantial increase in its garbage disposal costs. In order to reduce the amount of garbage to be managed, and hence to control its costs, the town introduced what is known as the "Bag Tag Program". This programme limits the number of bags of waste, of a uniform size, to four per household. Each household is required to purchase a "bag tag" that is affixed to the waste bag, without which it will not be picked up by the waste-disposal truck. The price of these tags in 1991 was $1 (Canadian) each.

The property right that is established by the town of Gananoque with this policy is the right to have a bag of refuse disposed of. Each household has the "right" to produce four bags of waste. No more than four bags will be collected from each household, and no bags will be collected that do not sport the appropriate tag.

What happens if a household wants to produce five bags of waste? Although the official "bag tag program" does not consider "trading" these rights to produce garbage, there exists no particular reason why this may not occur. If someone wants to produce five bags of waste then he or she would have to find someone who does not need all of their allocation, and then negotiate a suitable "price" for the transfer. Even though an "official" market has not been established by the policy maker, anyone can look outside on the refuse pick-up day to see if any neighbours are not using their allocation. Or, advertisements may be placed in local community centres requesting that a mutually-beneficial trade take place. Households requiring less than their allocated allowance are similarly induced to seek out potential customers for these rights.

Giving households a property right over their garbage creation has had a sizeable impact on the quantity of garbage produced by the residents of Gananoque. One estimate puts the reduction in household waste production in the neighbourhood of 42 per cent (Laplante and Lambert 1994, p. 169). The local government has estimated that the costs of disposing of the waste have been reduced by 25 per cent as a result of this policy. Another interesting measure of the success of this policy is the observation that shoppers in this area appear to have become more discerning when it comes to purchasing highly packaged products.

Characteristics of the Property Right

The right to produce garbage, while not officially transferable, may be easily traded to a nearby neighbour. Once buyers and sellers are identified, all that needs to happen is to set a mutually acceptable price for the right, and how the buyer of the right to an extra bag of waste is to transfer the waste to the seller of the right (remembering that no household can throw out more than four bags). The farther apart the participants to each transaction are, of course, the more costly the trade will be (which, naturally should be reflected on the agreed upon price). Thus, one could characterize this right as being relatively flexible as it is not subject to bureaucratic hurdles, aside from the no more than four bags per household constraint.

The right is divisible only insofar as every household owns four allowances, each of which may be "sold". The quality of title of the right is hard to evaluate in the sense that the right really resides with the household residence and **not** with the residents themselves. Thus, a resident would not hold title to the refuse allowance should he or she move from the relevant area. And, of course, the right will last for as long as this particular programme is in place. Given that municipal governments in Canada are elected every three years, durability may indeed be a concern. Lastly, the right, per se, is not very flexible in that it is defined as a bag of refuse of a particular size. To the extent that the right to dispose of four bags of waste essentially is attached to the actual domicile, as opposed to the residents therein, its flexibility is limited.

We might illustrate the characteristics of this particular example of (potentially) tradeable garbage rights using the by now familiar schema. As Figure 3.4 shows, this policy has a great degree of divisibility and exclusivity. Also, since there is no stated end for the policy, the property right may be classified as quite durable. The right, however, is not particularly transferable because of the restrictions existing in the programme. The quality of title of this right is also poor as it exists only insofar as people are residents of the community.

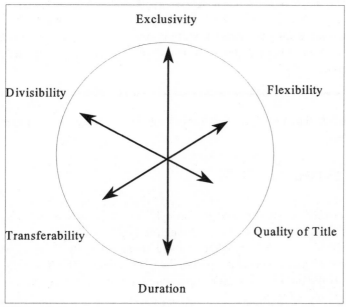

Figure 3.4

Sources: Laplante and Lambert (1994); Thivierge (1992).

The town of Gananoque is by no means unique in its approach to waste reduction. A few other municipalities have tried similar programmes to encourage individuals to throw out less. Note that an interesting feature of this type of programme is the fact that individuals have to find ways of changing their own behaviour to conform to the standard. Thus, this type of scheme targets directly the behaviour of the "polluter" rather than imposing standards on the community at large. One notable implication of any programme of this sort is that it will encourage the individual not only to reduce his or her own rubbish generation, but it may also encourage them to seek ways of circumventing the constraint. Researchers have uncovered evidence of two such ways of circumventing the intent of the policy. Some individuals have been found illegally dumping their wastes in vacant lots, neighbours' properties, or wherever. Others have cleverly figured out that their waste is constrained in terms of volume **not** weight - and hence have engaged in all sorts of "stomping" practices to reduce the volume of their refuse (Fullerton and Kinnaman, 1996)!

A third example of regulating a local environmental problem using tradeable property rights is found in the state of Wisconsin's Fox River experiment. This example is more aptly described as local as opposed to, say, national because the tradeable property right policy was introduced only in one well-defined part of the river.

Case 3.3: The Fox River Discharge Programme, Wisconsin, United States

The Problem

The Fox River runs northeasterly through east-central Wisconsin. The lower part of the river flows through a highly industrialized and populated area. Water pollution there stems primarily from *point* sources whereas, in the upper part of the river, pollution results mainly from *non-point* sources such as agricultural run-off. The focus here is on the Lower Fox river.

One part of the Lower Fox River drops rather dramatically, rendering it a highly desirable location for hydroelectric power generation. A series of dams was created to this end. An important source of industrial discharges is the 15 pulp and/or paper plants dotted along the lower river. Seven sewage treatment plants are also located here. Discharges from these two types of polluters are particularly high in organic wastes, which require large amounts of oxygen when decomposing. Thus, an important concern is the amount of dissolved oxygen left in the river to support fish and other aquatic life. As a result, one measure of the extent of pollution is the biochemical oxygen demand (BOD) occurring in the discharges into the river.

The BOD of the river improved significantly since EPA standards were implemented in the late 1970s. However, the problem of water quality persisted, particularly during periods of low river flow and high water temperature, both of which reduce the river's ability to absorb oxygen-demanding wastes. Some parts of the river had virtually no dissolved oxygen left.

A Property Rights Solution

In March 1981, the state of Wisconsin approved a plan which allowed the main dischargers on a 35 kilometre stretch of the Lower Fox River to trade the rights to discharge into the river. Ten pulp and paper mills and four sewage treatment plants were included in this programme. Each discharger was initially given an effluent waste load allocation specifying a maximum daily biochemical oxygen demand discharge level which would ensure the maintenance in the river of some chosen level of dissolved oxygen. Monitoring points were established along the river in which the BOD load and dissolved oxygen in the river were measured. Dischargers were given the right to discharge waste that increase the BOD of the river.

This particular type of private property rights scheme is an example of rights based on an *ambient* standard - measured in terms of the biochemical oxygen demand load and dissolved oxygen in the river at given receptor points. A discharger not able to meet its waste load allocation could enter into an agreement to buy credits from another discharger. However, trade between firms was complicated by the fact that it could not result in a purchasing firm exceeding the relevant ambient standard at the nearest measuring site. Indeed, suppose the selling firm reduced its effluent emissions by one ton, this did not imply that the buying firm could increase its effluent discharge by one ton since the impact of that increased effluent on the water's quality might differ from measuring site to measuring site. It would depend, for instance, on how close other dischargers are to the seller and purchaser, how deep the river was at their respective locations, and so on.

Only one trade appears to have actually taken place in this programme. The explanation lies at least in part in the complex administrative requirements and regulations associated with trading. For instance, trade could only occur if the purchaser could demonstrate to the state regulator that the increase in BOD discharges was needed. Need was defined very specifically as referring to either a new operation, increased production, or an inability to meet the specified waste load allocation even when using waste treatment facilities optimally. Thus, for instance, trades geared to reducing operating costs were **not** approved. Furthermore, traded rights only lasted for five years, much shorter than the lifespan of a typical pulp and paper mill operation or waste treatment facility. Dischargers thus faced considerably uncertainty as to whether they would be allowed to continue producing BOD waste that exceeded their waste load allocation. The process of approving trades was also a lengthy and costly one.

Characteristics of the Property Right

In this case the property right was established over biochemical oxygen demand discharges. Although the right was, in principle, transferable, many administrative criteria hampered the actual operation of this market. The quality of the title for the property right was also very poor, again largely because the value of the right was not well defined. The right was not very durable, since it lasted for only five years. Finally, the asset, the right to discharge BOD wastes, had some degree of flexibility in the sense that its value depended on and indeed varied in response to, the behaviour of surrounding dischargers as well as environmental conditions. However, once again because its duration was only five years and since its value was dependent upon the specific conditions at the seller's and purchaser's monitoring sites, this property right was really quite inflexible.

In this particular case, the schematic illustration of the six characteristics of property rights as they pertain to the Fox River experiment differs rather dramatically in comparison to the previous cases. As Figure 3.5 shows, the characteristics of this particular property right do not strongly reflect the "ideal" situation in virtually

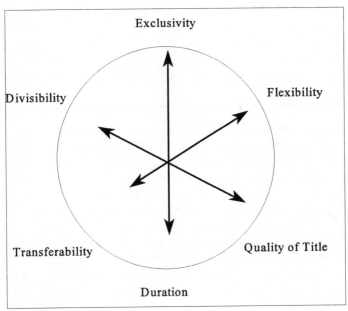

Figure 3.5

every dimension.

Indeed, if one compares this figure to those of the previous two cases one can see very clearly that the property right created for the Fox River falls short on a number of fronts. The only characteristic of the right that came close to being ideal is exclusivity. Aside from this, the right was not easily divisible - mostly stemming from the fact that it was based on an ambient standard. Because of imposed trading restrictions this right was not easily transferred and, indeed, was rather inflexible in terms of how it could be used by polluters. The duration and quality of

title of this right suffer from the same problems as other transferable
property right schemes for pollution.

Sources: Moore (1980); O'Neil (1983); Hahn and Hester (1989).

The Fox River experiment, in contrast to the other property-right schemes,
was based on an ambient standard rather than an effluent one. Thus, although
it was not very successful it stands as an example of how an ambient-based
standard may be operationalized.   Part of the reason why the Fox River
programme was not successful may well be attributable to the ambient-based
standard - since this increases the problems associated with trading. However,
many of the restrictions on trading imposed in this case did **not** arise because
of the ambient standard. Thus, we are left with some hope that better, more
flexible ambient-based schemes will be introduced in the future.
     Dealing with local pollution problems using tradeable permits is attractive
because the participants in the market are easily identifiable and hence
regulators may find it easier to construct such a programme. However, one of
the problems with local markets is that the number of participants **may** be so
small as to render impossible a "competitive" market, whereby all buyers and
sellers are price takers. One of the benefits of a competitive market is that
anyone willing to pay the price can buy permits.   In a market with few
participants one could observe one firm controlling which firms may purchase
permits, leading to distortions in how they are allocated. The issue as to whether
the permit market is competitive does not exist in the RECLAIM nor Bag Tag
programmes, while it was most certainly an issue in the Fox River experiment.
When the pollutant is national in scope, the likelihood of having too few
participants in the trading market is significantly reduced.

National Problems

Acid rain is both a national and an international problem, particularly when
countries are geographically close to each other. The experience in continental
Europe, for instance, provides a good example of how contiguous countries are
forced to cope with international pollutants. While Canada is clearly affected

by air pollution from the United States, and vice versa, these countries are so geographically vast that one might usefully consider the U.S. acid rain problem as being a national one. Consequently, creating tradeable property rights to help to improve the situation is a fairly straightforward policy. By contrast, creating property rights that may be traded internationally would be considerably more complex. The sulphur dioxide trading programme in the United States represents an interesting approach to dealing with the problem of acid rain.

Case 3.4: The U.S. Trading Programme for Sulphur Dioxide

The Problem

So-called "acid" rain first became a public policy issue during the 1970s when a number of studies began linking the degradation of forests, lakes and rivers to sulphur dioxide emissions. Sulphur dioxide (SO_2) is one of the main byproducts of coal-fired industrial plants. Indeed, in the United States, electricity generating plants account for over two thirds of the SO_2 emitted from point sources while representing only about 1,000 of the 18,000 or so known sources. Without policy intervention, plants would discharge as much SO_2 as they wished without considering its effect on others.

SO_2 emissions not only degrade the air and land in the areas surrounding the polluting source, but can travel across national and international boundaries making the problem of local, national and even international importance. With many of the electric utilities located close to the Canadian border, contributing significantly to the acid rain problems in that country, pressure to improve the situation came from inside and outside the U.S. boundary. Notice that, in this particular case, those who bore the cost of the externality were often not the same as those who enjoyed the benefits from the productive activity.

Various command and control type standards have been implemented over the past 25 years or so to reduce SO_2 emissions. For instance, the U.S. *Clean Air Act* of 1970 imposed more stringent emission rate standards on newly operating utilities. And, although overall standards were set for individual states, some jurisdictions experienced greater

---

success than others in attaining them. In fact, because SO_2 emissions can be carried with the wind, some states met targeted emission levels by allowing industries to build high smoke stacks. Local air quality was thus improved, at the expense of other jurisdictions. The fact that older plants continued to operate with dirtier technologies (using, for instance, high sulphur coal) contributed to the problem. Thus, SO_2 emissions continued to be on the political agenda through the decades of the 1970s and 1980s, prompting policy makers to look for a solution that would balance the public's need for electricity with its need for clean air and productive lakes and streams.

A Property Rights Solution

After reviewing and wrangling over a great number of proposals, the U.S. Congress and President Bush approved significant amendments to the Clean Air Act in 1990. These amendments introduced an extremely flexible and comprehensive trading programme in SO_2 emissions. This programme was implemented in conjunction with the existing ambient air quality standards in each region.

The property right introduced in the Clean Air Act Amendments (CAAA) takes the form of an allowance which gives the polluter the "right" to emit one ton of SO_2. All of the large coal-fired electricity generating plants in the United States must own a sufficient number of allowances to justify their emissions. Presently, some 111 plants located in the eastern and mid-western states are affected by this policy. Phase I of the policy took effect as of 1 January 1995. Every year each of the affected plants is allocated a number of permits based on a percentage of their 1980 output. The number of allowances or permits allocated is then ratcheted down each year. The goal of this policy is to reduce SO_2 emissions by five million tons in the first phase and an additional five million tons in phase II. Phase II of the policy begins on 1 January, 2000 and brings with it even tighter standards as well as including other, smaller plants into the programme.

An electric utility may decide to reduce emissions and use only the allowances allocated. Or, it may decide to abate emissions **below** allowable levels, in which case it can put its extra allowances up for sale on the allowances market. Firms that want to produce more SO_2 than their allocated allowances would support, must then purchase allowances from another firm. (A certain number of allowances are set aside each year to be auctioned in case any firm is caught short in any given year.) Firms are fined a significant amount of money for each ton of SO_2 emitted without an allowance ($2,000 per ton whereas the allowance will cost only a small fraction of this amount).

Information on the prices of allowances is difficult to obtain, due to the private nature of many of the transactions. At the auction of permits, held annually as a means for those utilities "caught short", prices have fallen rather steadily since 1994. In March 1996, for instance, the clearing price on the "spot market" auction was $66 for an allowance, whereas it was over $140 in September 1994. Part of the explanation for this phenomenon may rest in the larger than expected emission reductions due to abatement.

An interesting feature of this programme, making it one of the most flexible tradeable property right schemes, is that very few restrictions are placed on trades. Any plant/individual may purchase or sell allowances without the Environmental Protection Agency's (EPA) approval. Each state monitors trading activity, and, as would seem reasonable, the total emissions within each state must continue to conform to the overall standards previously set by the EPA.

One measure of the flexibility of this programme is the fact that the EPA does not even track the trading of allowances. Unfortunately, this means that it is difficult to obtain a precise measure of the amount of trading that has taken place in this market. The EPA, however, does keep track of the trading of allowances that are used by utilities in order to comply with the policy each year. Since March 1994, over 2,000 allowance transactions involving over 40 million allowances have been recorded by the EPA. Nearly 90 per cent of participating utilities have been involved in some kind of private allowance transfer.

Characteristics of the Property Right

Allowances to emit SO_2 are for the *exclusive* use of their owner, typically the electricity-producing utilities. They are *transferable*, with few restrictions on their ability to be sold. Each allowance is for one ton of SO_2, so they are quite *divisible*. As far as the *quality* of the title to these rights is concerned, it would appear to be well developed. However, the right itself does suffer from the same problem as all artificially-created assets in that its value depends crucially on the reliability and durability of the policy that created it in the first place. So, for instance, the right is durable only insofar as the *Clean Air Act* is not revised again to dismantle the programme. Finally, allowances are *flexible* in that they may be conferred by their owner upon anyone else who wishes to purchase them.

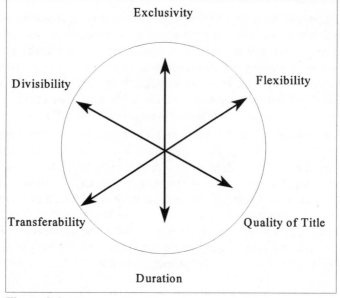

Figure 3.6

Sources: http://www.epa.gov/docs/acidrain/update3/allws.html

Again, using the schema developed earlier, we might visually categorize the SO₂ allowance property right as in Figure 3.6. The property right created by the allowance programme looks very similar to that of the RECLAIM scheme. The right is flexible, exclusive, divisible and transferable. The duration of the right may be as little as one year (although they can be hoarded for future use), which renders it less than "ideal".

Acid rain is a problem in many countries. While the approach in the United States has relied in part on private property rights, individual European countries seem to prefer taxes. The European Union has, however, devoted a great deal of time and effort looking into the possibility of having tradeable permits for the likes of SO₂ that could be traded throughout the community (Forsund and Naevdal, 1994). Because of the close proximity of international borders in Europe, solving the acid-rain problem really does require international cooperation. Since the 1970s, the transboundary migration of pollutants has been monitored across Europe. Scandinavia, for instance, **emitted** some 251 thousand tons of sulphur dioxide in 1991 while it **received** some 1,151 thousand tons (Hodge, 1995b, p. 124)!

International Problems

A number of pollution problems cross over international boundaries and thus require worldwide cooperation to resolve. Such international cooperation, however, may be extremely difficult to obtain, often necessitating compromises among countries with different goals. In many cases, the objectives of one group of countries, like the "developed" ones, differ substantially from another group of countries, like "developing" ones. Consider, for instance, the problems associated with rainforest deforestation where the conservation of forests imposes a greater immediate cost on Brazilians than it does for citizens of other countries. Another clear example of an international externality which requires worldwide cooperation to resolve it is the thinning of the ozone layer.

The possibility of using a permit trading scheme to deal with international problems has been raised in the literature. In particular, internationally traded carbon permits have been proposed as a way to implement emissions controls for greenhouse gases. Depending upon the criteria used for the initial allocation, such a system could provide substantial benefits to developing countries who could sell some of their rights to wealthier countries (Bertram, 1992). This possibility is but one of several outcomes that could arise if pollution rights are traded internationally. For instance, countries that share borders may find individuals on one side buying up and retiring pollution rights from the other side - in effect, they would be "buying" cleaner air. Such activities are quite likely to take place in contiguous countries like Canada and the United States, or France and Germany.

While an exciting possibility, setting up an international system of tradeable rights is an extremely complicated process and would require far more international cooperation than we have seen thus far. The hurdles that would have to be overcome are really quite staggering: standards would have to be set within each country concerning the monitoring and enforcing of the system; detailed rules would have to be established regarding domestic and international trades; and some kind of international tribunal would have to be created to deal with cross-border disputes. Furthermore, the question as to which countries would receive what initial allocation of rights is an extremely sensitive one since this initial allocation would be an important factor in determining the distribution of the *rents* associated with the scheme (Matsuo, 1997; Heal, 1992). Furthermore, when one takes into account the importance of carbon-based fuels in virtually every economy of the world, one gets a much clearer picture about the importance of the initial allocation of rights as well as of the magnitude of the vested interests that would be involved in such a scheme. Nevertheless, as technology advances and helps regulators to monitor compliance and trades and as countries become more experienced with tradeable permit schemes, the possibility of internationally traded rights becomes increasingly real.

For problems like ozone-layer destruction where the costs are borne worldwide and virtually every country contributes in one way or another to the problem (albeit to different extents), international cooperation is essential. Once an agreement is in place, it is then incumbent upon each of the signatory countries to implement the terms of the agreement in their own way. The United States, for instance, chose to implement a tradeable property right programme to fulfill its obligations to control ozone-depleting substances.

Case 3.5: Controlling Ozone-Depleting Substances

The Problem

The problems associated with ozone depletion are worldwide. Because of the widespread recognition of the importance of the ozone layer in protecting us from harmful ultraviolet radiation, an international agreement was sought to encourage the reduction of ozone-depleting substances. The 1985 Vienna Convention on the Protection of the Ozone Layer was one of the first formal attempts internationally to protect the ozone layer. However, it was not until 1985 (too late for the Vienna Convention) that it was discovered that the "hole" in the ozone layer had expanded significantly to a size comparable to the area of the continental United States! The Montreal Protocol of 1987 arose from the pressure that came about as a result of this finding. It laid out formal guidelines for the use of ozone-depleting chemicals. Particular attention was given to chlorofluorocarbons and halons, which are scheduled to be completely phased out by the year 2000. To meet its obligations under the Montreal Protocol, the United States implemented a transferable permit scheme for these substances.

A Property Rights Solution

Interestingly, perhaps because of the high degree of consensus internationally regarding the destruction caused by the thinning ozone layer, both the consumers and the producers of chlorofluorocarbons (CFCs) and halons are regulated. Furthermore, rather than just controlling the production of these substances consumers too had to be regulated because CFCs are recyclable. Consumers and producers were allocated an allowance based on 1986 usages, which is ratcheted downwards over time. All major consumers and producers are included in this programme.

A great deal of flexibility is accorded the transfer of these allowances. Not only can they be traded within consumer or producer groups, but allowances can also be traded between consumers and producers. Trades may also occur between producers in the United States and those elsewhere as long as the external producers operate in a country that signed the Montreal Protocol and meet other requirements as approved by the U.S. Environmental Protection Agency.

Characteristics of the Property Right

The property right associated with the production and use of CFCs and halons possesses a great deal of flexibility when it comes to transferability. The quality of the title of this property right is quite well developed. However, because these substances are scheduled to be completely phased out by the end of the century leaving any rights possessed at that time valueless, the right is not particularly durable. Nevertheless, the right does embrace a fair degree of flexibility during its lifespan in the sense that its owner may transfer the property right relatively easily to another producer or consumer.

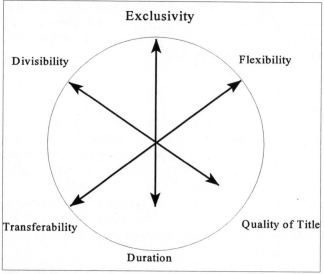

Figure 3.7

If we were to illustrate the characteristics of this particular property right scheme, it would look something like Figure 3.7 above. Once again, the tradeable right fares very well in terms of transferability, divisibility, exclusivity and flexibility, and not as well on the other two characteristics.

Sources: IUCC (31 January 1996), Climate Change Fact Sheets; Tietenberg (1995).

3.4 IMPLEMENTING PROPERTY RIGHTS: WHY AND WHY NOT?

What circumstances render the transferable property right solution an interesting one? Let's look at the five case studies to see if they provide any clues as to when one might expect this policy to succeed.

Of the five examples, three of them are successful, one cannot be fully evaluated because of lack of data (household waste), and one has clearly been less than effective (Fox River). Comparing the schema presented for each case we can see that in the Fox River experiment, the rights were much less transferable than in the other examples. The problem with the Fox River policy was that it contained many restrictions on the types of trading that could occur. Further, the targeted standard for this programme was a qualitative or ambient one, which necessarily adds a complication to the operationalizing of a tradeable property right scheme. Other restrictions, like requiring all dischargers to demonstrate to the satisfaction of the regulator that they needed the extra allowance, may have arisen from the inexperience of the regulators. These restrictions would have increased the costs of transacting in the market, hence reducing the incentive to trade. It seems a bit odd when reflecting on this case that firms were not allowed to purchase biochemical oxygen demand (BOD) allowances simply to reduce operating costs. One lesson learned from the Fox River experience is that the rights have to be easily transferred in order for the market to run well.

The Fox River situation also had many fewer participants in comparison to the number of participants in the other four examples. It is quite likely, therefore, that the market was just too small to generate enough interest in trading. For instance, if all of the facilities located along this 35 kilometre stretch of the river had similar technologies which is not unlikely, then the supply of and/or demand for BOD rights may be quite slim. Thus, the number of participants in the market and differences between them is important for the success of a tradeable rights policy.

Another feature of the RECLAIM and SO_2, programmes, in contrast to the other cases, is that the number of allowances are ratcheted down each year. In effect, this feature encourages participation in the allowance market by rendering the constraint that firms cannot pollute any more than their allowances will support, more binding over time. Firms are thus induced to go to the permit market to satisfy their requirements or to invest in cleaner technologies.

In addition to having easily transferable rights and a large number of participants in the market, what else would facilitate the use of the property rights solution? Looking at the successful cases we see that the right itself needs to be well defined in order to facilitate trading. This criterion was clearly met in the RECLAIM, SO_2 ozone-depleting substances and bag tag programmes. The right in the Fox River experiment, however, was not nearly as well defined - largely because of its reliance on a quality standard.

A comparison of the figures presented for each of the five tradeable property right schemes yields another useful observation. It appears as though the key to success for a property right programme is that the right be exclusive, divisible, flexible and easily transferable. Interestingly, the duration of the right and its quality of title are not nearly as critical. This observation is not so obvious if one were to examine tradeable property right schemes "in theory". So, while a property right created over some externality is a valuable asset just like any other asset in a variety of dimensions, it appears that a poor quality of the title to the asset does not reduce its attractiveness in any material way. A "conventional" asset, like a house or car, however would be affected by a weak ownership title. The reason for this difference between these artificially created assets and the more conventional assets lies in the fact that the transferable property right has value to the firm by virtue of the fact that it allows the firm to carry on with its activities using its current technology, at least in the short run. Depending on how likely it is that the tradeable right be renewed, the firm can use this short run to plan its alternative pollution abatement strategies. Thus, although tradeable rights may have a finite, and often short, duration they may well represent a successful policy. Because firms cannot switch instantaneously to cleaner technologies, the right to pollute at this moment in time has value even though it may not last for a long period of time.

3.5 FURTHER READING

A huge literature exists on externalities and property rights, most of which is written for and by economists. The classic article on property rights and externalities is by Coase (1960) which is reprinted in Dorfman and Dorfman (1993) and Oates (1992). Scott and Johnson (1985) provide an excellent discussion in a nontechnical way about property rights and natural resources and along with Scott (1989) is the source for our discussion on the characteristics of property rights. For a nice overview of property rights and the environment we suggest Bromley (1991). We recommend Barzel (1989) for a detailed discussion of property rights in general and Libecap (1989) for case studies of problems associated with property-rights regimes. If you're interested in detailed case studies of how specific environmental problems have been resolved we suggest Arnold (1994). Panayotou (1993) also provides many good examples of the environmental challenges we face and how people have gone about solving them.

Up-to-date information on the U.S. RECLAIM, Sulphur Dioxide and Chlorofluorocarbon trading programmes can now be found in the World Wide Web. The South Coast Air Quality Management District publication entitled *AQMD Advisor* is available at http://www.aqmd.gov/pubinfo and provides an excellent update of RECLAIM activities. Information on the SO_2 programme is found in the U.S. Environmental Protection Agency's web-site: http://www.epa.gov/docs/ acidrain/update3/allws.html. An excellent summary of transferable property rights is found in Tietenberg (1995); and Schmid (1995) in the same volume: *The Handbook of Environmental Economics* gives a nice synthesis of some of the issues raised when applying property rights to solve environmental problems. Portney (1993) provides a nice overview of the evolution of environmental regulations in the United States.

4

Property Rights for Natural Resources

4.1 CHARACTERISTICS OF NATURAL RESOURCES

Natural resources include all aspects of the environment - the forests, the oceans, the air we breathe, mineral deposits, soil and freshwater - virtually anything that is not human-made and is of value to us. Natural resources can be *renewable*, having the potential to be self-perpetuating, or *nonrenewable,* which can only be depleted.

Renewable and Nonrenewable Resources

Sometimes the distinction between renewable and nonrenewable is not so clear. For instance, old-growth forest in parts of North America is not considered a renewable resource despite the fact that trees may return even after an area has been logged. The time it would take for an old-growth forest to be restored can be over a hundred years, rendering it essentially a nonrenewable resource. The fact that renewable resources have the **potential** to be self-perpetuating or regenerative also does not preclude the possibility that they can be exploited or depleted to extinction. For instance, the great auk, a flightless sea bird found in the north Atlantic, once numbered in the millions but was exploited to extinction by the middle of the nineteenth century.

Whether a resource is renewable or not has little to do with its scarcity. Some "renewable resources" can be very scarce like the tuatara lizard in New Zealand or the giant panda in China, while some nonrenewable resources can be abundant. For example, silicon is nonrenewable but is hardly scarce since it accounts for 28 per cent of the earth's crust! Mineral desposits, like most nonrenewable resources, are also *stationary* in that their location is fixed, and are *storable*. By contrast, fisheries are *fugitive* resources which can and do move, often making their management more difficult.

Although the total amount of a nonrenewable resource can only stay the same or decrease, the amount that can actually be used by people may **increase** over time due to new discoveries or better ways of exploiting existing reserves. The proven reserves of bauxite (a mineral used for making aluminium) are over ten times higher today than they were in 1950 (Moore, 1995). By contrast, many renewable resources are much more scarce today than they were, say, 50 years ago.

Sustainability

Whether a resource is *sustainable* or not refers to whether it is self-sustaining (but not unchanging) over time. It is closely related to the concept of *sustainable development* which requires that we manage our planet so that future generations have the potential to be as "well off" as the current generation. Sustainable development does **not** mean preserving the environment or natural resources in the same state as we found them - an impossible goal with 6 billion people on earth! In fact, almost every environment on earth is affected by human activity. Whether we manage resources explicitly or not we affect our environment. For example, the world's oldest national park, Yellowstone in the United States, has a very different environment now to what it had in the past despite a "hands off" and noninterference policy since 1969. Today, the elk population greatly exceeds its prehistoric level and the park's ability to sustain them (Budiansky, 1995). Sustainability requires that we leave the environment in such a way that it can adapt and provide for the needs of future generations.

Frequently, the management of resources may be in conflict with the notion of the sustainable use of a resource. In some cases, the "owners" of natural resources - whatever the property-rights regime - may even consider exploiting the resource to extinction. For example, an owner (private or public) of an old-growth forest may find it beneficial to cut down all the trees and put the money from the sale of the timber in the bank. Indeed, if the value of a natural resource, such as from a forest or a fishery, **always** grows or regenerates at a rate less than the rate of interest we would receive at a bank an incentive exists for the owner to exploit the resource to extinction. In this case, converting the trees in the ground or fish in the sea to dollars in a bank will generate a higher return than sustainably managing the resource. This, however, may not be desirable from society's perspective if people value the resource other than for its value in consumption. For instance, many individuals value the existence of blue whales, the largest animal on earth - a value that has nothing to do with the consumption of whale as oil or meat.

To the extent that nonrenewable resources can only be depleted, their use cannot be said to be sustainable. However, the known reserves of many nonrenewable resources (iron, manganese, boron) will last several hundred years at current rates of consumption (Goeller, 1995, pp. 316-317). Further, the price of several important non-fuel minerals - such as nickel and aluminium - has fallen relative to the cost of most other goods over the past few decades (Myers *et al.*, 1995). This does not, however, imply that the availability of nonrenewable resources is not an important issue. Indeed, the existence of cheap sources of energy in the form of hydrocarbons such as coal, oil and natural gas has been very important in improving the standard of living of literally billions of people. Further, the *second law of thermodynamics* or the entropy law states that energy is ultimately transformed into heat which becomes so diluted or dissipated that we can no longer use it. This law means that, sooner or later, we will be forced to use more and more higher entropy resources with less potential energy. In terms of immediate environmental challenges, however, the problems are almost entirely directed to renewable resources.

Surprisingly, self-perpetuating resources are also those which pose the greatest problems in terms of sustainability. The depletion and over exploitation of renewable resources arises because they are also *common-pool resources* - where the yield or harvest of one person affects the exploitation of everybody else and where it is difficult to exclude others from using the resource. The difficulty of excluding people from using common-pool resources has hindered the development of private property rights - a regime which compels owners to consider the effects of their actions on themselves in the future. In some cases, community rights and state rights have developed to ensure that resources are used sustainably. Where property rights do not exist, resource users exhibit virtually no concern for the future, and over exploitation almost always arises.

No property-right regime - private or otherwise - guarantees that resources will be managed sustainably. Community-managed irrigation projects can and have led to the salinization and reduced fertility of soils and community-managed forests in Japan may not have been used as well as they could have been (Kitabatake, 1992). Privately-owned land in the mid-west of the United States was mismanaged in the earlier years of this century and contributed to the Oklahoma Dust Bowl of the 1930s. During the years of the Dust Bowl, much of the top soil over large areas of land literally blew away due, in part, to soil erosion from cultivation, leading to the exodus of tens of thousands of farmers and their families.

Resilience

Related to the concept of sustainability is the idea of the *resilience* of natural resources. Resilience refers to the capacity of a natural resource, population or ecosystem to absorb or adapt to change without being dramatically altered following some kind of shock, human-made or otherwise (Holling, 1973). For example, the accidental introduction of rats into New Zealand around 1,000 AD by the first settlers from Polynesia, and then later by Europeans in the nineteenth century, decimated the populations of many unique flightless birds. In this case a small change to the ecosystem had a large impact on important natural resources because the rats ate the eggs of the birds which nested on the ground. The lack of resilience of natural populations is a contributing factor to extinctions. The hunting of the blue whale ended in the 1960s, yet the population is still endangered with some recent evidence suggesting that only 2,000 blue whales remain (Myers, 1993). A similar story is true of the passenger pigeons that once numbered in the billions in nineteenth century North America. Excessive hunting led to a dramatic decline in numbers and although flocks of the birds were observed after hunting was prohibited, the bird became extinct in 1914 (Williams and Nowak, 1993).

The concept of resilience applies to ecosystems, communities and even human populations. The arrival of Europeans in the Americas in 1492 along with many diseases which did not exist in the western hemisphere beforehand, and the exploitation of native populations led to a wave of death on a scale unparalleled in human history. In what is today the United States and Canada, at least 7 million native North Americans lived in 1492; by 1900 fewer than 400,000 were left (Thornton, 1987). Over this time period, many cultures and peoples ceased to exist.

For many resources, their resilience cannot be determined until after a shock. Sometimes the shocks can be catastrophic and can neither be planned for nor controlled. For instance, we can do little to prevent a collision of the earth with a large meteor. Such an event, as suggested in the *Alvarez Hypothesis*, provides an explanation for why dinosaurs became extinct about 65 million years ago

(Jablonski, 1993). However, the human destruction of natural habitats, and the over exploitation which imposes large shocks on natural populations, can be managed. Although the resilience of ecosystems cannot be predicted well, resilience is important. Understanding the functioning and interrelationships of natural populations is essential in order to balance the costs and benefits of exploiting natural resources. In turn, effective management is a function of the property-rights regime and requires consideration of both the sustainability and resilience of natural resources.

Rents

Natural resources are managed because they yield a value to the people who use them. In hunter-gatherer societies or in subsistence agriculture, resources may simply be used to provide food, clothes and shelter to live. We may also use natural resources for the sheer pleasure and joy they give us, as from whale watching or from a visit to a national park. Where natural resources are used for their *consumptive* value - what they can yield in monetary terms - as opposed to what they can provide in non-monetary benefits, an important concern is to get the greatest benefit possible from the scarce resource. To achieve this goal, we should try to minimize the cost of harvesting or extracting a resource, whatever the level of output. To do otherwise would be wasteful. Thus, in addition to considering the sustainability and resilience of a resource, we should also fix the harvest or yield to maximize the present and future returns to the users. In other words, we should get the best return available from what nature has given us.

These goals for the exploitation of natural resources, if achieved, lead to what is known as "rent" maximization. Rent in this sense is not what we pay every month for an apartment but is simply what we have left over, in monetary terms, after paying all the costs involved in harvesting a resource. The surplus is called rent. Some of this surplus can be attributed to the management or harvesting skills and technology employed by people who use natural resources, and rightly belongs to them. However, a part of this surplus or rent is due to the scarcity of the resource. Unlike a manufactured product where production can increase if demand increases, the supply of many natural resources cannot. This limited supply, fixed by nature, means that the people lucky enough to exploit the resource can receive a surplus - called a resource rent - which is entirely due to its scarcity.

Resource rents play an important role in explaining how natural resources are managed. For resources where no one can be excluded, the existence of resource rents will encourage more and more users until this surplus no longer exists. When the surplus is finally dissipated, the resource is no longer being harvested at the appropriate output. The loss or dissipation of resource rents where there is no property right has led people to change the structure of property-rights regimes so as to get the best return from these natural resources. In some cases, private property rights may be the preferred regime, while in others community rights or state rights or even a mix of rights may be desirable. Different property rights may lead to different resource rents and distributions of the rents. Resolving how to maximize the resource rents over time and determining who gets what share of the resource rent are fundamental issues in resource management.

4.2   PROPERTY-RIGHTS REGIMES

To address the difficulties associated with the over exploitation of natural resources we need to understand the merits of different property-rights regimes. Solving the problem of the misuse of natural resources is **not** simply a matter of creating private property rights. In some situations, community rights may need to be enforced or encouraged while in others private rights may actually need to be subsumed (with just compensation) by the state. For example, when some countries created national parks, the property rights of previous owners were abrogated. In such a case, the exercise of private rights - for instance, the burning of trees - may be incompatible with the aim of preserving unique environments. The preferred property-right regime or mix of regimes is the one that provides the best means and incentives for people to help internalize externalities in a cost-effective, equitable and sustainable way.

Open Access

The arrangement that can lead to more externalities in common-pool resources than any other is open or free access. Open access describes a situation where no controls are placed on how much firms or individuals can consume or produce and no restrictions exist on the number of firms or individuals. Essentially it is where no property rights exist over the resource in question. More accurately we can describe open access as a "free for all" where people are able to exploit the resource as they see fit. Not surprisingly, open access leads to the over exploitation of our natural resources, a case where "everybody's access is nobody's property" (Bromley, 1989). Often described as the "Tragedy of the Commons" (Hardin, 1968), the real tragedy is **not** that resources are owned in common but that resources are owned by nobody.

Many of the world's global environmental problems arise from open access. No one owns the atmosphere so it is often used as a repository for wastes and pollution. Disputes between countries in Europe over acid rain and in North America between Canada and the United States have their root cause in firms treating the atmosphere as free to all. Polluting firms that would not consider dumping their wastes on the land of a neighbour may quite happily discharge the same wastes into the air. The sad story of the American buffalo which was hunted almost to extinction is an example of what may happen under open access. In the case of the buffalo, the herds were "owned" by the Indian tribes of the Great Plains of the United States and Canada. The invention of repeating rifles and the arrival of the railway in the west brought in non-indian hunters who could slaughter large numbers of animals. The resulting free for all almost led to the extinction of the buffalo and the annihilation of the way of life of the Lakota, Kiowa and other native peoples (Josephy, 1994).

In today's world, fortunately, only a few instances of true open-access regimes remain for natural resources. One example is fishing on the high seas outside the 200 nautical mile exclusive jurisdiction of coastal states. One of the cheapest ways to fish is to lay driftnets, nylon nets at or near the surface attached to buoys. Anything that isn't small enough to swim through the net gets caught. Those fish or marine mammals that cannot be sold are simply dumped overboard after the net is hauled onto the boat. Sometimes these nets can be several kilometres in length and can catch literally thousands of fish. What's even worse, sometimes the nets are lost at sea and continue "ghost fishing" for years, becoming "walls of death" indiscriminately catching and killing all creatures they entrap. The fact that driftnet fishing will ultimately damage future fishing is not important to some fishers because if they do not catch the fish someone else will. Further, the value that we may place on the mere existence of such animals as dolphins and porpoises killed by these nets is also not considered. The principal reason for the over exploitation of fisheries is not high seas driftnet fishing, as such, which has been banned by the United Nations, but a lack of adequate property rights over the oceans, and the incentives that this has created to overuse marine resources.

Limited-user open access

Open access has been transformed in a number of ways to prevent over exploitation of natural resources. For example, in some fisheries the state has imposed total harvesting limits enforced through restricted fishing seasons and prohibitions about where people may fish. Whenever the expected total catch approaches or exceeds the total allowable, the fishery is closed and no further harvesting is permitted. Such rules may be collectively called *regulated open access* (Wilen, 1993).

In addition to restricting the total harvest or yield, states have restricted the **number** of users or persons exploiting a resource so as to increase the exclusivity of the property right. A property-right regime which limits the number of users and total yield is called *limited-user open access*. Depending on the regulations, the transfer of access and withdrawal rights to the resource may be permitted. Sometimes the rights have a well-defined quality of title and may even be durable in the sense that the right exists for as long as the owner. Limited-user open access regimes, however, fail to limit the production or consumption of individual users such that the property right is **indivisible**. Plenty of examples of limited-user open access exist, including many developed fisheries where licences have been established which restrict the number of vessels allowed to fish. These licence restrictions sometimes limit the size of vessels, the fishing gear that may be used, or even the location where fishing is permitted.

Limited-user open access represents an improvement over open access and protects the resource. Unfortunately, it often fails to change the incentives faced by users. Given a fixed total harvest, fishers have every interest to catch their fish as quickly as possible before someone else does and the fishery is closed. This leads to additional investment in bigger or faster vessels and more sophisticated ways of harvesting fish. Over time these investments increase the fishing power of vessels and the costs of fishing but do not increase the **total** amount of fish caught. This competition among fishers results in an overcapitalized fleet that can easily catch far more than the total allowed, making the management of the fisheries even more difficult and wasting valuable resources. Excess investment and overcapitalization also help to create a system of management where regulators are loath to reduce the total catch because fishers need minimum quantities of fish to be able to stay in business. The collapse of the Atlantic Canada ground fisheries in the early 1990s was, in part, due to over harvesting in a limited-user open access regime (Hutchings and Myers, 1994). This catastrophe means that 500,000 metric tonnes less fish were caught in 1995 than in the mid 1980s while tens of thousands of fishers and fish-processing workers are now unemployed or under employed.

The problems of limited-user open access exist in a variety of situations. In the United States, many people may have drilling rights for oil and gas but ownership of the fuel is assigned only after it is brought to the surface, the so-called "rule of first capture". Because oil is typically found in a common pool, the more that is pumped out of one site the less it can be extracted from others. Further, because the cost of extraction is inversely related to how much oil is left in the ground, every incentive exists to pump oil as fast as possible to take advantage of lower extraction costs today. Once again, the costs imposed on others are not fully taken into account by well owners. The problem is made even worse because rapid extraction reduces the total amount of oil recovered from an oil field. For example, in the West Texas oil fields in the 1920s the total oil taken from the ground was just 20-25 per cent of the total available; with controlled extraction as much as 85-90 per cent may have been extracted (Libecap, 1989).

Despite the problems associated with limited-user open access some successes do exist. Where users of a resource have a very limited opportunity to increase their harvest or production, controlling the number of participants may be sufficient. The regime may work well if users are small in number. This is because limited entry may lead to cooperative rather than competitive behaviour as the number of users becomes smaller, leading to greater exclusivity for those who have access to the resource. Indeed, in some fisheries limited entry has improved the overall management of the resources. For example, in the British Columbian roe herring fishery, fishers have mostly welcomed regulations which restrict them to defined areas in an effort to manage the fishery (MacGillivray, 1986).

State Rights

State rights refer to property rights that are vested in a central governing authority. These rights can co-exist with other property-rights regimes. For instance, in most countries the "state" or collective citizenry owns the fishery resources up to 200 nautical miles from the shore. If the state chooses not to exercise its rights to manage the resource it can allow open access. It could also limit entry and have a limited-user open access regime or create private ownership of harvesting rights to fish. The property regime that emerges is at the forbearance of the owner of the resource, the state.

A state property right is not necessarily a bad thing. Indeed, the hunting preserves of feudal kings such as William I of England represent an early form of conservation of forests for hunting purposes. Later, public forests were developed in seventeenth century France to ensure an adequate supply of trees for the construction of naval vessels (Scott, 1955). During the Theodore

Roosevelt administration (1901-1909) the U.S. federal government was the prime mover in the conservation of public land. Since the creation of the world's first national park, Yellowstone National Park, in the United States, many states have created parks and conservation areas for places of natural beauty and/or areas with important or unique flora and fauna. Few people would argue against states exercising these rights.

State rights have also been used to create externalities and override the individual rights of its citizens. For example, the Chinese government's "Three Gorges" plan to dam the upper reaches of the Yangtze will dispossess up to 1.5 million people from their homes, change their way of life, force them to lose traditional rights to natural resources, and will destroy unique areas of natural beauty. States have also attenuated or abrogated common-law traditions of private land owners to the detriment of the environment. For example, in Canada the Province of Ontario overrode a supreme court injunction and passed an act so that a pulp and paper mill could continue polluting a river although this imposed considerable costs on downstream users (Brubaker, 1995).

The principal weakness of state rights is that they tend to be inflexible to changes in both the environment and society. This inflexibility is exacerbated when citizens are denied the right to express their views through control of the media, state intimidation or even a lack of political democracy. Inflexible rights can also mean that socially undesirable projects that would never arise if land were privately owned may occur where land is state owned. A comparison between the state of the environment in the former East and West Germanies illustrates some of the problems that can arise when state rights predominate. The situation in the former Soviet Union provides us with a stark reminder of the problems that may accompany dominant state rights.

Example 4.1: The Poisoning of Russia

Rules and regulations to protect the environment have existed since the Bolshevik Revolution of 1917. In fact, the Soviet Union was one of the first countries, in 1949, to set up an administration to monitor the compliance of air pollution standards. Unfortunately, many of these regulations were ignored and enforcement was minimal. The overriding objective in the Soviet era appeared to be to meet production and output targets - whatever the cost. Little or no incentives existed to consider the costs to the environment or to clean up polluted areas.

By the late 1980s, Russia and some of the former Soviet Republics faced some of the world's worst environmental challenges. In Moscow, fewer than 30 per cent of industrial polluters have installed purifying equipment, most of which is ineffective and is often turned off during night shifts. It is estimated that pollution is the direct cause of one fifth of all illnesses in Muscovites. In Russia as a whole, concentrations of sulphur dioxide and total suspended particulates are almost three and five times greater than exist in the United States. This pollution explains, in part, a death rate from respiratory diseases in men almost three times higher than is found in the world's five largest economies - the United States, Japan, Germany, France and the United Kingdom. Indeed, Russian men now have a life expectancy that is closer to that of developing countries than of a developed nation. Equally as important, the total emissions of air pollutants may have risen by as much as 40 per cent from 1970 to 1990 while over the same period total emissions fell by some 35 per cent in the United States. In the former Soviet Union almost 75 per cent of all surface water was classified as polluted in 1989 while almost a third of all water discharges in the Russian Federation is completely untreated.

Sources: Bernstam (1995), Feshbach (1995); Feshbach and Friendly (1992).

The pollution and environmental degradation prevalent in Russia also exists, to a lesser extent, in countries with a mix of property-rights regimes. In Canada, a confederation of ten provinces and two territories, forests comprise about 45 per cent of the land area. Each province has jurisdiction over its own forests with most of them owned and managed by the provinces themselves. The environmental challenges facing Canada's forests include a concern over the cutting of old-growth forests, clear cutting of large areas of land which can negatively affect wildlife until the mature forest comes back, and balancing recreational and commercial uses of forests. The fact that the forests are publicly owned clearly does not ensure that exploitation is always in the public interest.

Example 4.2: Alberta's Boreal Forests

The boreal forest covers about a third of the total area of Canada and is one of the largest contiguous forests in the world. In the late 1980s, the Alberta government conceived of a plan to reduce the province's dependence on oil and gas production and increase employment by turning the boreal forest into pulp and paper. The total forest area planned for felling was the size of Great Britain and in latitudes where it can take literally hundreds of years for mature forests to grow back. These forests not only have value by being a net absorber of carbon dioxide in the atmosphere, a "carbon sink", but are desired in terms of recreation and for maintaining the traditional way of life of native peoples.

The benefits of the forestry development include an increase in direct employment of about 4,000 people and an investment in construction of new plants and the expansion of existing pulp and paper mills worth some $U.S. 3 billion. The costs to the people of Alberta include almost $U.S. 1 billion in government loans and infrastructure used by the mills - subsidies that amount to about a quarter of a million dollars per permanent job! Despite such large subsidies, it appears that a government cost-benefit analysis of the projects was never undertaken. In fact, the Alberta Forestry Minister in 1989 is on record as saying, "If God had wanted cost-benefit analysis, he could not have built the world in seven days." The environmental costs of the mills include not only the loss of the forests and habitat but also water discharges which will include dioxins and furans, and are highly toxic. Given the size of the subsidies by the Alberta government to the forest companies, it is highly unlikely that the scale of the development would have been as great if the forests had been privately owned.

Sources: Pratt and Urquhart (1994).

The cutting down of forests with little thought to the costs involved is repeated elsewhere in the world. The basic problem is the same - the forests are publicly owned and managed by officials who often provide concessions to companies in return for just a small share of the value of the trees. Unlike community or private rights, under state rights the persons making decisions about the management of natural resources do not depend upon the resources for their livelihood. The separation of decision-making authority from the people who benefit from the resources can lead to inferior management. Further, states may be "captured" by vested or special interests which becomes more likely the greater the consumptive and market benefits of natural resources.

The short-term logging rights traditionally given to companies, particularly in developing countries, also provide little incentive for the harvesters to replant. The problems of tropical deforestation are compounded by government incentives and subsidies to convert forests into agricultural land. For example, until the 1980s the Brazilian government provided subsidies to cattle ranchers to convert forests into ranch land (Browder, 1988). These subsidies over the period 1975-1986 amounted to over $U.S. 1.5 billion and have resulted in cattle ranches occupying almost three quarters of the **cleared** land in Amazonia (Park, 1992). Because pasture growth cannot be maintained without considerable investment, many ranchers have found it cheaper to clear new land and move the cattle to new pastures after five or ten years. Indeed, clearing forests is one of the cheapest ways to acquire land in Brazil because of the right known as *direito de posse* which gives title to squatters who live on and effectively use unclaimed public land for more than five years. In a country where land prices rose 11 per cent / year in real terms between 1970 and 1985 (Andersen *et al.*, 1996) this provides considerable incentives for clearing of forests.

State rights for forests and land can also mean that objectives other than the optimal management of natural resources dominate. For example, the governments of Indonesia and Brazil have funded large-scale migrations of the poor from relatively overpopulated parts of their countries into the rainforests. The Indonesian Transmigration Policy has been particularly devastating on tribal people in Irian Jaya, on the western part of the island of New Guinea, who have been dispossessed of their communal rights to land. Further, these migration policies have not, in many cases, led to sustainable land management practices (Park, 1992).

The combination of state rights and population and economic pressures means that worldwide tropical forests are being denuded at a rate of almost one per cent per year (Sedjo, 1995). If these rates of deforestation continue, the world's tropical forests will be greatly reduced within our lifetimes. Unfortunately, the beneficiaries of tropical deforestation have little incentive to change their current practices and the decision makers rarely bear the cost of their actions. These costs include a loss of species of fauna (25 to 50 per cent of the world's species live in tropical forests), the destruction of native cultures, soil erosion, loss of water quality and an increase in greenhouse gases in the atmosphere. If, however, citizens of temperate countries wish to ensure the continued existence of tropical forests, they must be prepared to pay for it. For example, transfers in excess of $U.S. 9,000/ha. from the rest of the world will be required by the year 2010 to make it worthwhile for the Brazilian government to conserve the rainforests in the Amazon (Andersen *et al.*, 1996).

Solving these and other natural resource problems is not simple. As much as anything, it requires an active participation in decision-making by all stakeholders - the owners of the resources, those who bear the costs, as well as the beneficiaries. Sometimes the environmental and resource problems may require a shift in the structure of property rights from state rights to community or private rights or to a mix of several property-rights regimes. In other cases, it may involve a change in the political economy of the country and active participation by citizens in decisions that affect resources managed by governments.

The fact that elected officials and bureaucrats may make decisions against the public interest does not mean that state rights are always undesirable. Several examples exist where state rights to resources have been used to improve overall welfare. The more important are non-market benefits and the greater geographical dispersion of these benefits, the larger should be the comparative advantage of state rights. Without state rights and the powers of exclusion that a government can impose, many of the wilderness areas in North America would not be protected appropriately. State rights have enabled the United States to increase the area of land in national parks 20 fold since the turn of the century, and the area of land in the National Wildlife Refuge System five fold since 1950 (Nelson, 1995). These changes reflect the desires of most Americans. Changes in state rights are also taking place in other countries. Colombia, at least on paper, has confirmed native title to about a third of its territory in Amazonia (Prance, 1993). Following the assassination of Chico Mendes in 1988, the founder of the Brazilian Rubber Tappers' Union who lobbied for native rights and sustainable use of the Amazon, the Brazilian government set up reserves in the Amazon. Rubber tapping and the extraction of fruits and nuts are permitted in the reserves but logging of trees and deforestation is not.

It appears that state rights work best when non-market benefits predominate and are dispersed across a population, mechanisms exist for people to express their preferences to the state, no prior claims by individuals or communities exist over the resource, and when the state has the means to enforce rights and the costs of exclusion are high.

Community Rights

One of the earliest forms of property rights is community rights over an environment or a collection of natural resources. Many hunter-gatherer and pastoral people have *de facto* rights over the land they use in the form of community rights. These rights often prohibit persons outside the community from using the resources, and set rules for how the resources should be exploited by members of the community. Depending upon the type of resources and community, these rights may provide a large measure of exclusivity. Community rights are unlikely, however, to be alienable or transferable outside the community or divisible and often lack the quality of title and flexibility found with private property rights.

Numerous examples of community rights can be found throughout the world. Many pastoralists in the Sahel region have community rights over grazing land. Such rights also exist in the alpine areas of Switzerland, Peru, Ecuador and Bolivia. Community rights are found in fisheries throughout the world, in irrigation projects in Asia, Africa and the Middle East, and for forests and woodlands in countries such as Japan. The conditions which characterize successful community rights include: well-defined geographical boundaries for the resource, rules of access and withdrawal that are accepted by the community and which are tailored to the resource and institutions, some monitoring and enforcement of rules with sanctions against transgressors, resolution mechanisms for disputes among members, and rules that cannot be superseded by a higher level of governance (Ostrom, 1990). Community rights will also have a greater chance of success the smaller the number of community members, the better the technology to exclude non-members, the greater the importance of the resource to the survival of the community, the more important are mutual obligations and ties among members, and the ease with which transgressors can be detected (Wade, 1987).

Example 4.3: The Forests of Nepal

The forests of Nepal are found in the foothills and mountains of the Himalayas. They provide an important source of fuel for people, timber for building, and fodder for livestock. The forests also protect the integrity of watersheds and water supplies, help prevent soil erosion, and constitute an important ecosystem. In 1957, the government of Nepal nationalized all forests - the stated aim was to better protect the forest resources. Unfortunately, the immediate effect was to encourage private owners to transform forests into farm land so as to avoid the land being appropriated by the state. Merely decreeing a state right does not create a property right unless exclusivity can be enforced. Following the nationalization, communities which previously managed local forests for the benefit of themselves no longer had the same exclusivity and flexibility that they once had. The change in the incentives encouraged further over exploitation of the forests. .

The realization that a lack of community rights to forests was exacerbating the problem of deforestation led to changes in policy in the late 1970s and early 1980s. Since 1979, the creation of community forest groups has been encouraged, and legal tenure for local forests has been given to some village development committees. In addition, up to a third of Nepal's forests appear to be managed by informal and/or unofficial community groups. In the case of Nepal, the state has realized that community rights are probably a more effective way of managing forests resources than state rights.

Sources: Bromley and Chapagain (1984); Bromley (1991); Pradhan and Parks (1995).

The replacement of community rights by state rights has also occurred elsewhere, particularly under colonial administrations. For example, community rights in Mali's Niger River delta were undermined by French administrations and after independence all natural resources became state property. State ownership has led to a "take-over" of the more productive resources by powerful individuals and groups, and to open access to resources that were previously managed by communities (Swallow and Bromley, 1995; Moorehead, 1989). Given that exclusivity requires monitoring and enforcement, state ownership can resemble open access in countries where the state has very limited financial and human resources (Grafton, 1997).

Sometimes different rights can exist contemporaneously for the same resources. In the Swiss grazing commons, community rights and private property exist for alpine pastures used by livestock. A comparison of the efficiency of private and community rights suggests that private alpine pastures yield a higher average output than their common counterpart. This difference between the property regimes is **not** necessarily because the community pasture is overgrazed, as we may expect in open access, but is possibly due to under investment in improvements to the land relative to private pasture (Stevenson, 1991). Whatever the possible merits of private pasture, community pastures have for centuries ensured the sustainable use of a fragile ecosystem in an equitable way. Further, the pastoral alpine system developed under community rights allows farmers to support 30 per cent more livestock than they would otherwise (Wohlfarter, 1965, p. 8).

Example 4.4: The Swiss Grazing Commons

> The tradition of community rights in alpine pastures goes back at least as far as the arrival of the Alemanni who colonized the Swiss Alps over the period 300 to 1,000 AD. As the population increased, open access to pastures changed into community rights to persons with a family lineage in a specific area. Eventually, community rules changed to make community rights even more exclusive. First, individuals were only allowed to graze animals on the community pastures that had overwintered in the valley. Later, communities limited the total number of animals on the common pasture and the total number of persons with community grazing rights.
>
> Depending on the community, a host of other rules must be followed by users of the common pasture. These rules are made by the community and for the community where members are both the beneficiaries and enforcers of the rules. Access to the alpine pastures is limited by a season set by the community which determines the date livestock can start grazing on the alpine pasture and the date they must be returned to the valleys. Input rights have also developed which restrict the total number of animals that each member of the community can graze. These rights, however, are transferable and can be bought, sold and rented among members of the community. Transferability ensures that individuals with the highest value use from the pasture have the opportunity to increase their share of the total livestock on the common pasture.
>
> *Source:* Stevenson (1991).

Many other examples of community rights exist. Most are traditional rights that have existed for generations despite efforts by states to undermine them. Going back at least as far as 1743, villages along Japan's coast have exercised some control over fishery resources including their management and conservation. More recently, management has focused on sedentary species such as shellfish and seaweed which do not migrate from one village to another, and enhancement of fishing grounds through the use of artificial reefs and human-made spawning grounds. Most members of these communities believe that community rights have reduced competition and conflict among fishers and have reduced total fishing effort (Yamamoto, 1995). The Penan of Sarawak in

Indonesia are peacefully fighting against commercial logging companies which have been given rights to log their traditional lands. The response by the Indonesian government has been to arrest protesters and entrench the rights of the companies. In Brazil, the Gavoies people successfully fought against resettlement and appropriation of their land and have taken control of the collection and sale of Brazil nuts on their land (Park, 1992). Similarly, since 1989 the Kayapo of A-Ukre in the Amazon have been selling Brazil nut oil to Body Shop International.

In some cases, community rights have been devised in the recent past to deal with environmental degradation and over exploitation. One example is the allocation of fishing rights among fishers in Alanya, Turkey (Berkes, 1986). Fishing pressure led a cooperative in the 1970s to set up a system to minimize competition and assign fishing sites to individuals in an equitable way. Such a system was a definite improvement over the previous open access.

Community rights, in the appropriate setting, also offer a means to internalize the externalities that arise from local common-pool resources. In Senegal, following nationalization of land in 1964, community rights to rangelands were undermined which, coupled with droughts, led to severe overgrazing. A solution to the problems has been to establish pastoral units collectively administered by groups of villages. These units have legally-valid community rights to watering areas and grazing land (Vedeld, 1992). The success of pastoral units, and indeed all community rights, is based on the effectiveness of the rules and conventions set for all members.

In general, natural resources and environmental problems overlap communities and affect many people, especially in urban populations. Thus, the environmental problem sometimes may be too large and communities too disparate for community rights to effectively control externalities. Further, technological change which increases the divergence between private and community interests is likely to destabilize community rights. Past and current conflicts between artisanal fishers and fishers employing larger and more sophisticated vessels and gear in southeast Asia (Weber, 1994) are, in part, a reflection of the break-down in the exclusivity of community rights in the presence of technological change.

Where communities cannot enforce rules, where the boundaries of natural resources are not easily delineated or where it is difficult to exclude non-members from access, community rights are likely to be ineffective and other property-rights regimes may be preferred. By contrast, community rights will tend to have a comparative advantage where mechanisms exist to reflect collective interests and preferences, individual costs of exclusion are high, the ratio of non-market to market benefits is high, and the rate of technological progress in exploitation is relatively low.

Private Rights

A standard economic prescription for the externalities that arise from the use of common-pool resources is to create private property rights and internalize the costs that individuals impose on others. The overriding advantage of private rights is the potential to transfer or alienate a share of resources. This allows resource users, who can generate a higher return from the resource, to acquire a greater share of its yield and thus increase aggregate benefits. The appropriateness of the "private property rights solution", however, depends on the cost of exclusion relative to the benefits of private rights, the institutional setting and equity considerations.

The likelihood of finding private property rights for common-pool resources regimes depends on the technology available to enforce the rights and the value placed on the particular goods and services arising from the resource. For example, in the past territorial ownership over the seas was limited to the furthest distance a cannon could reach if fired from land. Today, ownership of fisheries extends to 200 nautical miles from the coast - a change made possible because countries can now effectively monitor by sea and air their coastal resources. Parallel to these technical changes has been a shift in property rights over fish. In the past, fish at sea belonged to anyone who could catch them whether or not they were "owned" by the state or crown. Now vessels can be and are arrested hundreds of kilometres out to sea for infringing fishing regulations, such as took place in the 1995 "Turbot War" between Canada and the European Union in the northwest Atlantic. Improvements in technology for enforcing property rights has meant that private property rights, which would have been impossible even 50 years ago, can be contemplated in ocean fisheries.

Despite the fact that the costs of exclusion remains relatively high in fisheries, private property rights have been introduced in a number of countries with considerable success. These private property rights are mostly in the form of individual transferable quotas (ITQs) which represent a harvesting right to a fixed quantity or a proportion of the total allowable catch of fish. They have been introduced in several countries including Canada, United States, Iceland, Australia and New Zealand in response to crises in fisheries. These crises have arisen because fisheries have either been open access, regulated open access or limited-user open access. A private property rights approach limits each fisher to a fixed amount of fish which can then be increased or decreased by trading with others. The output constraint provides incentives to fishers to minimize their costs while transferability allows for a *decentralized* solution because lower-cost fishers can purchase property rights from higher-cost individuals and increase their share of the total harvest.

Case 4.1: Individual Transferable Quotas In New Zealand's Fisheries

The Problem

Until the introduction of individual transferable quotas (ITQs), New Zealand's fisheries were either open access, regulated open access or limited-user open access. By the early 1980s, some important fish stocks had been depleted following the rapid expansion of the fishing fleet in the 1970s. To help limit catches to a sustainable level and maximize the resource rent from its fisheries, the New Zealand government introduced a comprehensive system of ITQs in October 1986 covering 30 species.

The Property Rights Solution

The introduction of ITQs has led to significant improvements in the fishing industry. The overall impression from both the industry and the government is that the economic performance of fishers has improved. The industry-funded New Zealand Fishing Industry Board states that ITQs have increased the economic benefits from the fisheries while ensuring their continued sustainability. This view is confirmed in an index of competitiveness, using industry costs and revenue, which suggests that competitiveness improved by about 20 per cent in the first five years of ITQs. Surveys of individual fishers also reveal that a significant number believe that ITQs have improved product quality by reducing the race to fish. In the important snapper fishery, 40 per cent have changed their handling and processing of fish so as to receive a higher price for their product in Japan. In the hoki fishery, New Zealand's largest in terms of weight, ITQs appear to have led to more specialized fishing and improved product quality. In addition, more than twice as many fish are now caught outside the spawning season and spawning grounds. Private rights have also led to greater involvement by fishers in decision-making in their fisheries. Some fishers have clubbed together and pay for full-time research on their stocks while others have even requested a reduction in the total allowable catch because of concerns about overfishing. ITQs also seem to have helped the sustainability of the fisheries. In 1993, only 13 out of 149 fish stocks were below desirable levels and of these 13 stocks most are being rebuilt with lower catches.

Despite considerable successes, problems persist. It seems that ITQs may have increased the dumping of fish at sea and have led to so-called "high grading" whereby lesser valued fish are thrown overboard so as to maximize the return per unit of quota. There have also been some well-publicized violations of ITQ regulations. Further, disputes have erupted between the Maori, New Zealand's native people, and the government over the allocation of fishing rights. Negotiations eventually led to a landmark agreement in 1992 which transferred over $U.S. 300 million in assets to the Maori people and gave them close to 40 per cent of the New Zealand commercial fishery. In addition, the Maori will be allocated 20 per cent of the quota of any new fish species placed under ITQs.

Characteristics of the Property Right

ITQs represent a harvesting right to catch fish in designated areas over a one year period. This right is divisible and transferable among New Zealanders although limits are placed on the proportion of the total quota that can be owned by any one individual or company. To ensure exclusivity, the government has devoted considerable time and resources to monitoring the fish landed and processed, and reconciling these records with quota ownership. Penalties for fishing without quota are severe and can include the confiscation of the boat and quota as well as fines for the captain and owner(s). The enforcement of regulations is helped by the fact that 85 per cent of New Zealand's harvest is exported and the small domestic market reduces the opportunity for over-the-counter sales. Flexibility is built into the system by allowing fishers the right to land up to 10 per cent above their quota in any one year, with the extra landings deducted from the following year's quota. To provide incentives for fishers to land fish they have caught, but for which they do not have quota, the government allows fishers to keep 50 per cent of the value of these landings. The intention is to ensure that fish caught is landed and recorded but not to provide an incentive for fishers to fish without quota. ITQs are now denominated as a share of the total allowable catch rather than as a fixed quantity of fish. Proportional or share quotas have placed a greater burden of risk on fishers because with quantity quotas the government had to buy quota from fishers to reduce the total allowable catch following a decline in the stock.

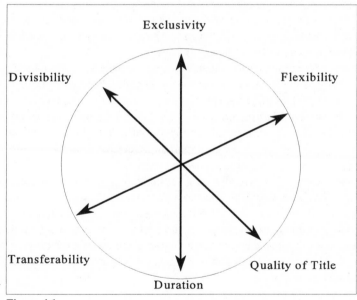

Figure 4.1

Sources: Annala (1996); Grafton (1996a).

The relative success of ITQs in New Zealand's fisheries is repeated in Australia, Canada, the United States and Iceland when the property right is viewed as exclusive and adequate monitoring and enforcement exists. For example, some evidence indicates that efficiency increased in Canada's Pacific halibut fishery because of ITQs (Grafton *et al.*, 1997). In Australia's southern blue fin tuna fishery and the herring and capelin fisheries of Iceland, ITQs have coincided with a reduction in the number of fishing vessels while in other fisheries they have been associated with an increase in profitability (Grafton, 1996a). Despite these successes, ITQs are viewed with suspicion by some fishers. The rationalization of fishing fleets with ITQs has inevitably led to a fall in employment in fish harvesting. In some fisheries, transfers of quota have meant that certain regions process fewer fish which has had negative consequences on some small communities. Further, there is concern by some people that fishers have received valuable assets in terms of ITQs without paying the owner of the resource for the privilege of catching fish. Some of these concerns can be addressed by modifying the nature of the property right. It is also possible to take a share of the resource rent from the owner of the ITQ and give it to the owners of the fisheries (Grafton, 1995 and 1996b) as well as impose restrictions on transfers of quota across regions, if necessary.

In fisheries where monitoring and enforcement have not been adequate, a lack of exclusivity in the right has prevented the expected benefits of ITQs from being realized. Although private property rights by themselves will not solve many of the problems in fisheries, such as declining fish stocks, the poverty of artisanal fisheries, and international fisheries disputes, they do offer a means to increase the resource rents from an important renewable resource (Grafton *et al.*, 1996).

Private property rights have also been applied to improve the common-pool problems associated with nonrenewable resources. In the United States, ownership of oil and gas occurs only after the resource has been pumped to the surface so rights do not exist over the resource *in situ*. Because many oil fields will have several persons or firms with sub-surface rights over parts of the deposit, an incentive exists to pump as much oil out, and as fast as possible, before someone else does.

Example 4.5: Unitization of U.S. Oil Fields

In the United States ownership over oil and gas occurs after the resource reaches the surface. Anybody with sub-surface rights over an oil field has the right to pump as much oil as fast as they can and whenever they please. This is similar to open access, or at best, limited-user open access, for a common-pool resource. Consequently, oil is pumped out of the ground much too fast. This rapid pumping increases extraction and storage costs significantly and also reduces the total amount of oil taken from the field. Further, it has led to situations where although close to 90 per cent of the world's oil wells were in the United States in 1980, they provided **less than** one sixth of the world output!

One way this common-pool problem has been addressed is with the unitization of oil fields. Unitization involves all individuals and firms with sub-surface rights getting together and agreeing to let a single producer extract the oil, with the net revenues being apportioned among all owners at a fixed proportion. Sometimes when all parties cannot agree on how the net revenues should be apportioned, a subset of the owners of the sub-surface rights may agree to one party extracting the oil with a given net revenue share to all contracting parties. The benefit of unitization can be enormous. In one oil field alone in 1960 unitization could have resulted in increased oil recovery worth $U.S. 285 million. In general, the recovery rates of oil from early unitization can be between two and five times more than in oil fields without controls on production.

Despite its benefits, unitization occurs much less frequently than one might expect. The principal problem hampering unitization stems from the fact that all parties must agree on the appropriate share of the net revenues. Firms which own the sub-surface rights have only a small amount of objective information about the value of the drilling rights of others, but have a great deal of information about the value of their own drilling rights. To encourage unitization, the U.S. government provides special terms for oil leases on federal land if the field is unitized; in the state of Oklahoma, unitization is compulsory whenever a majority of persons with the drilling rights, weighted by the area over which the rights are held, are in favour of it. The state of Texas provides the least incentives and not surprisingly has the smallest proportion of total production from unitized fields.

Sources: Libecap (1989); Libecap and Wiggins (1985).

Unitization represents one way that individuals with private rights can mutually benefit from the exploitation of a common-pool resource. Another way is illustrated by the pumping of water out of the west basin of southern California. Originally, owners of land had the right to pump as much water as they wished from their own land. Eventually, over pumping endangered the water pool and increased the chances of salt-water contamination. This problem provided an incentive to landowners to pump as much water as possible while the resource was still available. In response, landowners got together and formed a water association and used the courts to solve the over pumping problem. In time, a contingent contract was signed whereby landowners agreed to limit their pumping provided that 80 per cent of all other persons with water rights also agreed. These contracts have become legally binding and are monitored by the association (Ostrom, 1988).

Private rights can be used in a number of different ways to help solve common-pool problems. In the case of fisheries, governments have created private harvesting rights - rights that improve the returns from the resource. In the case of U.S. oil fields private rights do not exist over the resource *in situ* but collective action, sometimes with government encouragement, has led to improved use of the resource. Private rights will be most useful where resources are valued mainly for their commercial value, the costs of excluding other users is relatively small, divisibility and especially transferability are possible, and the quality of title is well defined.

Achieving the Right Mix

We have separated the different property-rights regimes into a number of categories so that we can assess their relative merits for managing natural resources. In reality, many natural resources are managed in a way that combines aspects of different property right structures. Choosing the right mix of private, community and state rights to address environmental problems is not easy. Often, the mix of property-rights that develops is a function of past institutional arrangements, as well as present needs. An interesting mix of private and state rights is conservation trusts that are becoming increasingly important in the preservation of valued habitats in many countries.

Example 4.6: Conservation Trusts in the United Kingdom

Conservation, amenity and recreation trusts are nongovernmental organizations that have the aim of conserving important habitats and environments. The trusts often have relatively narrow objectives and may focus on particular areas or species. For example, The Royal

Society for the Protection of Birds owns some 180,000 acres of land, most of which encompasses important nesting sites. Until recently, the Butterfly Conservation kept secret the site of its reserves to keep the butterflies safe from unscrupulous collectors. The land holdings of the conservation trusts include woodlands, marshes, bogs, heaths and grassland. The principal objective of land ownership by trusts is to maintain specific wildlife and/or ecosystems.

The trusts carry out the mandates of their members by educating and informing the public as well by the purchase and management of land for conservation purposes. They differ from environmental pressure groups in that they actually take on or share the responsibility of land and wildlife management. Collectively the trusts number over three million members and employ over two thousand people. The biggest is the National Trust which is one of the largest landowners in the United Kingdom, playing a key role in the preservation of historic building and sites. The National Trust also has a special status with the state and the power to own land such that it cannot be transferred to anyone else without an Act of Parliament. In addition to the special status of the National Trust, the state also provides on average about one third of the income of independent trusts. Partnerships between trusts and local governments and private landowners also contribute fundamentally to the trusts achieving their objectives.

Sources: Dwyer and Hodge (1992); Hodge (1995b).

Conservation trusts are also important in North America. One of the largest is the U.S.-based Nature Conservancy, which had over 700,000 members in 1994, and has purchased land in Canada and the United States totalling more than 22,000 square kilometres - an area greater in size than Wales. In the case of the Nature Conservancy and other environmental trusts, the land purchased is sometimes given to both public and private conservation groups. Thus, conservation trusts provide an important way that individuals can collectively, without direct state assistance, conserve sensitive and unique habitats. These trusts represent a mix of property-rights regimes where private rights are used collectively by non-profit organizations, sometimes in collaboration with governments, to achieve environmental objectives. Such a mix, however, may not always be the "right mix" from society's perspective. Some conservation trusts' objectives may be so narrow as to limit other environmental benefits.

For example, managing habitat to maximize the number of a particular species for hunting purposes (such as ducks) may have a negative effect on the populations of other species (such as fish).   In other cases, important environmental or societal goals may be ignored if they fall outside the mandate of the trust or organization.   Further, there are likely to be high fixed costs associated with the management of conservation areas which suggests a coordinated approach is desirable and that state rights have a role to play in realizing the net benefits from some natural resources. Thus, state rights are likely to be part of a mix of regimes to manage natural resources which provide multiple non-market benefits over a dispersed population.

Putting Rights in Practice: Biodiversity

An important mix of property rights has been established to protect *biodiversity*. This term comes from the words biological diversity and represents the incredible variation that exists in all living things across species and across individuals. Although the actual number of species on earth is not known, a widely-cited estimate places the number as high as 10 million (May, 1988). This variation or diversity is, strictly speaking, not a natural resource but a characteristic of natural resources. Diversity is considered important because a lack of variation in ecosystems can reduce their resilience (Holling *et al.*, 1995) and long-term sustainability - also known as the *contributory* value of biological diversity. Further, biodiversity is important for those humans who may value it as an end in itself - its *existence* value: and, because genetic diversity provides the "building blocks" for the human species, we may need it for our survival and well-being - the *commercial* value of biodiversity. For example, biodiversity may allow us to develop even higher yielding varieties of a crop like rice which is resistant to diseases and pests; or to develop cures for diseases like cancer.   Because species loss is irreversible, reducing biodiversity limits the options available to us whether they be to see rhinoceroses in the wild or to find a cure for AIDS.

Species extinctions occur regularly even without human intervention. Sometimes, however, extinctions happen *en masse,* as with the cretaceous extinction of 65 million years ago which eliminated the dinosaurs. The largest in terms of species loss was some 220 million years ago when as many as 96 per cent of the then living species disappeared (Jablonski, 1993). One problem we face today is that a growing human population and the increasing utilization of natural resources are placing greater burdens on habitats which, in turn, negatively affect biodiversity. According to the International Council for Bird

Preservation, about 20 per cent of all bird species are either extinct or are at risk of extinction. In this century alone, over 100 extinctions of animal species have been **documented**. The principal causes of the extinctions, in descending order of importance, have been species introductions, habitat destruction and hunting. Most of these extinctions have taken place on island habitats with unique species. Changes to isolated or island environments render native species particularly vulnerable because they are unable to migrate elsewhere and because they exist nowhere else. Globally, the International Union for the Conservation of Nature and Natural Resources considers that some 6,000 animal species are threatened in some way, of which about 1,200 are considered to be in immediate danger of extinction unless changes occur in the causal factors affecting the species.

Perhaps the most difficult question of all is to determine how much biodiversity is desirable. Humans only directly use a tiny fraction of the world's species, at most 0.1 per cent (10,000 species out of 10 million). This small proportion suggests that losing a few hundred or even thousands of species may have little impact on human welfare. The reality, however, is that we do not know what the consequences of species loss might be. If certain wild grasses had, by chance, gone extinct a few thousand years ago we might never have been able to domesticate rice, wheat, barley or oats - grains that play an essential role in feeding most of humanity. The potential also exists to have captive breeding programmes in zoos and wildlife parks and maintain genetic banks for fauna and flora. Some of these programmes have already saved certain species from extinction such as the wisent (European bison) and the Arabian oryx (Foose, 1993). Unfortunately, such programmes cannot be implemented on a large scale to conserve biodiversity due to the literally millions of species about which we currently know nothing. Thus, except for at most a few hundred species, the surest way to conserve biodiversity is to manage critical habitats wisely.

One problem that we face is to balance the benefits of biodiversity with the costs of its conservation. Not all habitats can or should be preserved, and the costs of not exploiting certain natural resources may be very high for the poor in low-income countries. If we cannot save all the species under threat, which ones should be given priority? There is no easy answer to this question. Some people believe that species should be valued by their existence value which would mean that pandas would probably be valued higher than worms. Others suggest that the value of a species is determined by its uniqueness or difference from other species. Some economists have suggested that the money spent on conserving biodiversity should be related to the probability of success in saving the species (Weitzman, 1993). Whatever the criteria, it seems that public policy has been directed to saving species which resemble humans in either size or characteristics (Metrick and Weitzman, 1996).

The fact that at least two thirds of the world's species are located in tropical countries also begs the questions of not only the appropriate level of biodiversity but also of who pays and who benefits from this diversity? Clearly all of us can benefit from cures for cancer but for people in low-income countries, who have access to neither primary health care nor clean drinking water, their priorities may lie elsewhere. For people with few options and little to eat, the costs of preserving biodiversity today - the inability to use important natural resources such as timber or increase the area of land under cultivation - will almost certainly outweigh any potential future benefits of biodiversity. To achieve the goals of biodiversity, and to do so in an equitable way, the persons forgoing development or the use of natural resources must be compensated in some way. In other words, there must be some return on the investment in preserving biodiversity to those bearing the costs, otherwise it will not take place. This incentive-based approach will probably be more effective than punishing countries which use their natural resources and threaten species diversity. Where states see a return from protecting species, such as Zimbabwe has in terms of wild elephants, populations have increased (Swanson, 1993). Where nations do not expect a return, little or no investment in protecting species or biodiversity will occur. This dilemma led to the Convention on Biological Diversity.

Example 4.7: United Nations Convention on Biological Diversity

The Convention on Biological Diversity came into force in December 1993 following discussions at the 1992 Rio de Janeiro Earth Summit. The convention seeks to ensure biological diversity, the sustainable use of natural resources, and the equitable sharing of the benefits of biodiversity. The convention has been signed by both poor and rich countries and entails benefits for each. Above all, it allows the free trade of genetic resources - a commercial value of biodiversity - while providing ways for richer countries to finance biodiversity conservation.

The convention has 42 articles in its main text. Article 3 of the convention specifically recognizes the right of countries to exploit their natural resources as long as this does not negatively affect other nations. Article 8 asks signatories to preserve biodiversity by establishing preserves, protecting endangered species, and ensuring the sustainable use of natural resources. It also recognizes indigenous knowledge that may lead to advances from the use of species and encourages the sharing of the benefits acquired from such knowledge. Articles 9 and 15 collectively allow access to genetic resources, considered to be owned by the state in which they reside, provided that the terms are mutually agreed upon between contracting parties and that access requires informed consent of a country. Article 16 requests technology transfer to promote biodiversity such that biotechnology will flow from richer to poorer nations, and genetic resources and knowledge about sustainable use of biodiversity will flow from poorer to richer countries. Articles 20 and 21 outline a system for financing biodiversity which recognizes the need for payment to countries for genetic resources that may have a commercial value.

Sources: Gollin (1993); Reid *et al.* (1993).

Prior to the Convention on Biological Diversity, Costa Rica signed an agreement with Merck - a U.S.-based pharmaceutical company - to provide chemical extracts from Costa Rica's wild plants, insects and micro-organisms in its conserved habitats. In return, Merck agreed to provide funding of $U.S. 1.135 million for the costs of biological prospecting, to pay a royalty on any commercial products developed from the genetic resources, and to help develop a drug research centre in Costa Rica. The signatory for Costa Rica was not the government but its National Biodiversity Institute - INBio - a private but non-profit organization created by the Costa Rican government in 1989 with financial assistance from foreign donors. INBio's biological prospecting and agreements represent an important mix of state, private and community rights for conserving biodiversity.

Example 4.8: Biodiversity Prospecting and Costa Rica's INBio

For its relatively small size (just over a third of the size of England), Costa Rica has a wide range of habitats from near desert to tropical rainforest located at sea-level to as high as 3,500 metres. This variation and tropical climate means that it has about 4 per cent of the world's total number of land species: a number of species many times more than that which exists in Canada, a country almost 200 times the size! INBio was established to help document some of this diversity, facilitate its access, ensure the preservation of all of its collections, and encourage the sustainable use of Costa Rica's genetic diversity for the benefit of its citizens (Reid *et al.*, 1993). These goals mean that it is one of the first organizations to be involved in the study, conservation and sale of genetic resources. Individuals or companies using the collections and information supplied by INBio explicitly recognize that Costa Rica has property rights over its genetic diversity, as promulgated in Costa Rica's 1992 Wild Life Protection Law. The contracts signed by INBio with Merck and other parties state that some of the research will take place in Costa Rica and that royalties will go to managing national parks and the ministry responsible for the conservation of natural resources. This creates another incentive for conserving Costa Rica's wildlands and helps provide the financial resources to accomplish this objective.

Sources: Reid *et al.* (1993).

Biodiversity prospecting, as practised by Costa Rica's INBio, provides a means for correcting the lack of property rights that previously existed over genetic resources. Not so long ago, firms and individuals could collect samples and benefit from human knowledge of species without the legal obligation to pay for them. Depending on the domestic laws of those countries which have signed the Convention on Biological Diversity, the use of genetic resources and indigenous knowledge now requires some form of payment. In a sense, genetic resources which were once considered a resource available to all and owned by no one have been transformed into state and/or private and community rights.

One weakness of genetic property rights is the difficulty involved in excluding users. This difficulty stems from the fact that it may be hard to prove a particular product comes from a specific genetic source in a particular country, and because excluding users from accessing genetic resources is problematic. Many examples exist of countries which have tried and failed to prevent access to their genetic resources. For instance, in the nineteenth century Brazil failed to prevent British plant collectors taking specimens of rubber plants which were subsequently introduced into Malaysia and turned into a commercial crop. Probably the best that countries with genetic resources can accomplish is to work with users by explicitly providing high-quality samples and information. This cooperation should encourage regulated access and will help provide a legal claim on products developed from the genetic resources and a return from biodiversity.

Establishing a right over genetic resources,so that countries can benefit from biodiversity, is an important step in moving to a more appropriate use of natural resources and the environment. However, to achieve the right mix of property rights and promote desirable levels of biodiversity is a more difficult goal. For example, transfers to national governments for genetic resources in wildlife conservation areas may do little to preserve biodiversity on private and communal land. If the state cannot monitor or control access and the users derive no direct benefit from biodiversity, the desired level of biodiversity is unlikely to be achieved. Further, the private value attached to biodiversity for use in pharmaceutical research may be very low. For instance, even in areas considered to be "hot spots" of biodiversity, the private value to pharmaceutical companies from conserving an additional hectare of land for its biodiversity is very small (Simpson *et al.*, 1996)

The recognition that conserving biodiversity requires new approaches has led to new management practices for wildlife. For example, the vicuna - a wild llama-like animal found in the Andes - competes directly for pasture with the domesticated llama and alpaca. By allowing local people to benefit from the sale of vicuna fibre, the Convention on International Trade in Endangered Species and Wild Fauna and Flora and the governments of Chile and Peru permit the people who most threaten the vicuna's survival to gain from its continued existence (Edwards, 1995). This approach does not guarantee the optimal level of biodiversity but it does combine state rights with community and even private rights in ways that lead to a better use of natural resources.

4.3   RIGHTS, REGIMES AND REMEDIES

Common-pool resources provide a means of survival and living to hundreds of millions of people. Ensuring that these resources are managed properly so that we and future generations obtain the most out of what nature has provided critically depends on the property rights that are assigned to them.

Successful property-right regimes create the right incentives and penalties to manage resources insofar as individuals are forced to consider the effect of their actions on others. For example, private harvesting rights in certain fisheries have improved the return from the resource in high-income countries. However, utilizing private rights in artisanal fisheries where communities have rules governing exploitation and where enforcement exists at the community level is probably not appropriate. Instead, protecting or encouraging community rights may be a better approach. Sometimes, property-right structures can be improved by direct government intervention while at other times the rights may evolve naturally over time. In still other cases, mitigating environmental and natural resource problems requires an improvement in one particular dimension of the property right rather than a complete change in regime. For example, with even only a small chance of eviction, a poor quality of title for land can result in short-term destructive practices by farmers (Mendelsohn, 1994). In many cases, an appropriate mix of property-rights regimes may be preferred (Grafton, 1997). Whatever the change, altering property rights will affect not only how the resource is exploited but who benefits from the rights.

4.4   FURTHER READING

Many good texts on the management of natural resources are readily available, most of which assume the reader has a background in economics. A very readable and interesting book for non-economists is Rees (1985). For people with economics training we recommend Pearce and Turner (1990), Tietenberg (1996), Randall (1987) and Dasgupta (1982). We also suggest Ciriacy-Wantrup (1968) for a nice review of the classification of natural resources. The concept of sustainability has generated a huge literature. An often cited book is *Our Common Future* prepared by the World Commission on Environment and Development (1987). Nice introductions to sustainable development, with plenty of examples, are given by Crabbe (undated), Elliott (1994) and Pearce *et al.* (1990). Pearce and Atkinson (1995) also provide measures of sustainable development. The relationship between ecological systems and sustainability with property-rights regimes is discussed by Costanza and Folke in the book *Rights to Nature* edited by Hanna *et al.* (1996). An article by J. Diamond in the August 1995 issue of the magazine *Discover,* which describes the history of Easter Island (Rapa Nui) provides a stark reminder of the consequences of not using resources sustainably. We also recommend Ponting (1991), Goudie (1994) and Nisbet (1991) for a review of the impacts of human activity on the environment.

The classic reference on resilience is Holling (1973) while Grafton and Silva-Echenique (1997) discuss the potential strategies for managing chaotic populations. Holling and Sanderson in the book *Rights to Nature* edited by Hanna *et al.* (1996) also provide a nice introduction to the dynamics of ecosystems. We highly recommend Josephy (1994) for an easy-to-read guide to the changes faced by native people in North America over the past 500 years.

Georgescu-Roegen (1975) has a thought-provoking article on entropy and economics. A useful reference on cost-benefit analysis is Hanley and Spash (1993). A very interesting perspective on the management of natural resources is in Budiansky (1995). The issues behind the scarcity of natural resources are nicely summarized in chapter 2 of Randall (1987). An easy-to-read introduction to rents and natural resources is given by van Kooten (1993, chapter 2). Krutilla (1967), which is reprinted in Oates (1992), is a classic paper on conservation from an economic perspective. We also highly recommend Scott (1955), especially chapter 3, for a history of conservation.

A number of books on topics covered in the chapter is also recommended. Park (1992) provides an introduction to tropical deforestation, Repetto and Gillis (1988) give an excellent collection of perspectives on the management of tropical forests, and Sedjo (1995) provides an up-to-date overview. Different perspectives on the causes of tropical deforestation are given in Brown and Pearce (1994) and Sandler (1993). Barbier *et al.* (1994) furnishes an-easy-to read overview, with examples, on biodiversity. For those interested in reading about species loss and its consequences we suggest Kaufman and Mallory (1993) and Perrings *et al.* (1995). An authoritative, if somewhat dated, reference on rights-based fishing is Neher et al. (1989). Berrill (1997) and Coull (1993) provide nice overviews of the world fisheries and their problems while Rettig (1995) details the different approaches to fisheries management.

Many case studies and examples of community rights are found in Hanna and Munasinghe (1995), Bromley (1992) and Berkes (1989). Ostrom *et al.* (1994) also provide a detailed analysis of community rights for a number of common-pool resources. A very useful book on property rights and natural resources is Bromley (1991). A nice collection of papers on the use of property rights for natural resources with an emphasis on institutions is given in the book *Rights to Nature* edited by Hanna *et al.* (1996). In this volume, we highly recommend the contributions of McCay, Ostrom and Schlager, and Eggertsson. Finally, a private property right perspective to solving environmental challenges is provided by Anderson and Leal (1991).

5

Controlling Environmental Degradation without Property Rights

5.1 CONTROLLING THE ENVIRONMENT

As a society, we are surrounded by the problems associated with pollution and environmental degradation. While property rights can solve many of these problems, it is clear that they also fall short of their goal on a number of occasions. It is also clear that governments are not always willing nor able to implement a property-right solution - even when this solution may be an appropriate one. Nevertheless, virtually every national government on the face of the earth takes credit for initiating, implementing or enforcing some type of environmental policy. If not private property rights then what? In this chapter, we focus on the "then what" part of this question. In other words we describe and discuss the various other types of policies or approaches that have been used to mitigate environmental harm.

One of the goals of policy makers is to try to encourage firms to emit only an "acceptable" amount of pollution. The property-rights solution creates clear incentives for firms to find the best, cheapest ways of reducing their level of emissions - since each unit of emissions **costs** the firms the market price of the allowance or permit. In technical parlance, the pollution *externality* can be *internalized*. When correctly implemented, the number of pollution permits or rights is set by the regulator so that the price of the permit on the market reflects the social cost of the unit of pollution "bought" by the permit.

The property-rights solution encourages firms to seek ways of reducing pollution in the least-cost way **and** it forces polluters to face all of the costs of their actions. Thus, firms are forced to conform to the internationally-accepted *polluter pays principle.* This principle, as its name suggests, dictates that polluters should be responsible for paying the costs of pollution to society. Although unquestionably a laudable goal, as we will shortly see, many of the policies currently in place do **not** conform to this notion.

One of the difficulties associated with determining the appropriate type of environmental policy is that often the best policy depends critically on the particular circumstances at hand. How much information does the policy maker need or have available to use? What are the characteristics of the pollutant itself? Where does the pollution come from? How many polluters are there? While we cannot possibly answer all of these questions, we try in this chapter to provide you with sufficient information so that you can assess the particular externality at hand and come up with your own well-reasoned list of potential, feasible, solutions.

Aside from using property rights, four other important means of encouraging the reduction of pollution are available to policy makers: standards, taxes, legal liability and international agreements. Let's turn now to a detailed discussion of these policies and the circumstances under which they are best applied. Particular attention is given to whether these approaches encourage the polluters themselves to seek out ways of reducing pollution, and to whether they conform to the polluter pays principle.

Standards

We begin our discussion with a review of the traditional approach to pollution control - standards. Standards are frequently referred to as a Command and Control (CAC) policy because they often dictate particular terms to the polluting industry or firm. They could dictate, for instance, that the firm may not pollute more than some given quantity, or that the firm must employ some given production technology. Examples of this type of policy abound. For instance, the U.S. *Clean Air Act Amendments* of 1965 set standards on hydrocarbon and carbon monoxide emissions from automobiles (Tietenberg, 1994, p. 409). Standards on automobile emissions in the United States have become increasingly stringent over the past 30 years. Automobile emission standards also exist in other parts of the world, such as in South and North America and the European Union; even the Russian Federation is attempting to implement such measures (Tietenberg, 1994, p. 412). Another type of standard was found in Britain during the 1950s and 1960s where clean air regulations were introduced banning the use of conventional coal, requiring the use of "smokeless" coal (Hodge, 1995b, p. 116). The British government is also trying to affect technology decisions with its *Environmental Protection Act* of 1990. Although this act imposes ambient air quality standards and waste emission standards on industries, it also compels the regulator to point out to the various polluters whenever technologies exist that are cleaner than those currently in place, as long as the new technology is not "excessively" costly (Turner *et al.*, 1994, p. 196).

Other types of command and control policies have sprung up in recent years because of our increased reliance on recycling. Minimum content laws can be found in at least 13 states in the United States concerning the amount of recycled material that must be used in products like newspapers, glass, telephone directories and plastics. A majority of states also have procurement laws in which government offices have to purchase some specified percentage of recycled products or use certain recycled products in state-funded projects (McClain, 1995, p. 237).

Standards are often imposed on firms or individuals irrespective of their particular circumstances. Recalling the analysis of Chapter 2 in which we discussed how one can determine an "acceptable" amount of pollution, standards force all (or virtually all) firms to behave in a set way. For instance, the U.S. *Clean Air Act* requires all cars to meet the same emission standards. These standards were set to meet air-quality standards in sensitive areas - like Los Angeles. All cars must meet the standards, however, irrespective of where they are driven. People in areas whose environment could tolerate more automobile emissions and who, therefore, are gaining very little from these policies are bearing the same costs as those whose environments are benefiting greatly from standards. One estimate puts the benefits of the 1975 and 1976 U.S. automobile emission standards in the range of $3.5 to $9.1 billion while the costs were calculated at about $10 billion (Tietenberg, 1994, p. 282). In other words, too much abatement may occur with standards. Thus, from the point of view of cost effectiveness, standards are often found to be less favourable than other, more flexible, policies precisely because of their rigid nature.

Standards are also costly to monitor and enforce by the regulator, and are costly to comply with by the firm. Their effectiveness in terms of pollution reduction depends critically on how the standards are set and enforced. Society benefits very little from standards that are strict in theory but rarely enforced - to which driving speed on busy motorways will easily attest.

Pollution standards are typically applied on a uniform basis across all emitters, suggesting that they are best used whenever polluters are very similar. Furthermore, imposing standards on a few manufacturers of certain pollution-generating products, rather than trying to control the users of these products, may also prove to be an effective strategy. For instance, since literally millions of automobiles are in existence, it makes sense for policy makers to target the relatively few automobile manufacturers and force them to introduce emission-reducing features - like catalytic converters to reduce hydrocarbon and carbon monoxide emissions, and engines that run on lead-free fuel - rather than trying to encourage individual owners to adopt certain measures.

Evidence appears to suggest that automobile standards have been quite successful at reducing emissions. In the United States, average emissions over the lifetime of an automobile have fallen dramatically since the 1960s. Carbon monoxide emissions, for instance, plummeted from some 19 grams per kilometre in the mid 1970s to about 8 grams per kilometre in 1984 (Tietenberg, 1994, p. 285); in California, where even more stringent standards apply, these emissions were projected to be just over 1 gram per kilometre in 1997 (*The Economist*, 14 September, 1996, p. 70). However, it has to be said that the 1973 OPEC oil embargo, which caused a large increase in the price of gasoline, dramatically affected Americans' love affair with the automobile. Bigger was no longer considered to be better. The average size of automobiles has fallen since that time and individuals, at least during the 1970s and 1980s, became increasingly concerned about fuel efficiency. This trend had a profound effect on automobile emissions. Nevertheless, the tightening of emission standards does seem to have improved the overall situation.

Standards are best applied to situations where the regulator can easily monitor their compliance. The fewer the number of firms that are subject to regulation, the better the chance that the standards will be successful. In addition to the number of firms, standards work better on *point* sources of pollution, rather than non-point sources. The pulp and paper industry as described in Example 5.1 illustrates this point very well.

Sometimes the social cost of an externality is just so high that our goal should be its complete elimination. In that case, the use of command and control policies may be the best way to effect this outcome. Completely banning the use of certain hazardous substances - like CFCs (after the year 2000) or the insecticide dichloro-diphenyl-trichloro-ethane (DDT) - may be better accomplished by a command and control policy than by other means.

While useful in certain respects, standards have a number of drawbacks. For instance, they typically do not provide strong incentives to firms to look for better, cleaner ways of conducting their activities. Once a standard is imposed, firms do not reap any benefit from, say, polluting less than the standard nor are they allowed to exceed it. Of course, when very stringent standards are used, as in the extreme cases where substances are completely banned from use, then firms have to find other ways of operating. But, again, firms do not gain from finding cleaner technologies; they are only induced to find a means of operating their businesses without the given substance.

Standards, to be effective, must be closely monitored. Firms simply have no incentive to comply with command and control policies unless there is a cost associated with non-compliance. The relationship between penalties for non-compliance and standards has been clearly shown for the pulp and paper industry (Laplante and Rilstone, 1996). The level of emissions in this industry was found to fall with the number of plant inspections and with the **threat** of inspections.

The pulp and paper industry worldwide is notorious for its impact on the environment. Water is used in almost every operation in a pulp and paper plant. Thus, among other things, this industry is one of the largest contributors to water pollution in those countries where the industry is economically important. The industry contributes significantly to the quantity of total suspended solids (TSS) in the water, and emits as many as 129 toxic pollutants. The operation of pulp and paper mills also contributes to air pollution. Both particulates and malodorous sulphur compounds are emitted at the pulping stage. Depending upon the type of boilers used in the pulping process, the emissions of particulates and sulphur dioxides may be rather significant. Finally, pulp and paper making also generates solid wastes which are typically disposed of in landfills (Luken, 1990, appendix A).

It is no wonder, then, that virtually every country regulates its pulp and paper industry. However, because jurisdictions differ tremendously in terms of size, water resources, population density and so on - all of which influence the magnitude of the pollution problem associated with the industry - considerable variation can be found in the success with which environmental regulations have been applied to pulp and paper mills.

Example 5.1: The Pulp and Paper Industry in Canada

The pulp and paper industry is one of Canada's most economically important industries, contributing about 3 per cent of its GNP. It operates some 150 mills in almost every region of Canada; and is the main source of employment for residents in about 175 different towns and communities. One of the difficulties associated with trying to control the environmental impact of this industry has stemmed precisely from the fact that its importance is concentrated in many communities.

The environmental costs of the industry, however, are borne by much larger and more diverse groups. For instance, the industry uses about 35 per cent of Canada's annual forest production, it is the largest industrial user of water, and the second largest user of electrical power. In 1971, Canada first regulated the pulp and paper industry's total suspended solid (TSS) discharges, its biochemical oxygen demand (BOD), and the toxicity of its emissions to fish. Various other dimensions of the environmental impact of this industry were regulated by provincial governments which frequently set standards that were stricter than those set by the federal government. Over the period 1971 to 1985 the amount of pollution discharged by the industry was reduced considerably while production increased by 31 per cent. Nevertheless, the industry has been the subject of considerable environmental concern and protests.

One of the problems facing the pulp and paper industry in Canada and its regulators is the fact that different firms are subject to different degrees of regulation. Typically, older plants are given much longer periods of time to comply with standards than are newer ones. In addition, the government appears to determine when and how each plant is to comply with these standards on a case by case basis - a time consuming and costly process. As if this were not enough, plants often do not meet the terms and conditions of compliance that were previously set. When faced with the threat of closure, and the impending economic devastation of a community, governments have not always been able to hold firm on their commitment to environmental standards. Thus, standards have had limited success in Canada.

Sources: Laplante and Rilstone (1996); Sinclair (1991).

Although it is most common to apply standards "across the board" and then, as the Canadian pulp and paper industry example illustrates, relax them on a case by case basis, this is not the only way to proceed. The pulp and paper industry in Sweden provides a nice contrast. All of the plants in Sweden are subject to individual standards concerning their biochemical oxygen demand, suspended solids and other measures of pollution. Thus, standards are set with specific reference to the characteristics of each particular firm. One reason why this approach is both feasible and fairly successful in the Swedish case while it is almost certain to fail in Canada, is that Sweden is geographically small relative to Canada. Since the effectiveness of standards is directly related to the amount of effort put into their monitoring and enforcing, and since it is much easier to monitor firms that are close in proximity to each other, it is not surprising that Sweden appears to have been more successful than Canada has been in regulating the pulp and paper industry (Brannlund *et al.*, 1995).

From the point of view of the polluter pays principle, standards do not fare very well. They do not compel the polluter to pay for the damage caused by his or her activities. They simply stipulate how much pollution can be generated, or they impose the technology that must be employed by the firm. Thus, standards do not compare well to, for instance, transferable private property rights, when judged from the perspective of pollution-reducing incentives.

In spite of their limitations, standards remain very popular with governments. Standards are appealing since they allow governments to appear to be in control of the situation. They are attractive to politicians who promise to "protect" the environment since standards represent a tangible action on the part of the government. One extremely useful characteristic of standards is their costs of enforcement are typically hidden from the public eye. Thus, politicians can seem at least to be doing something for nothing!

Charges

A popular way of curbing the pollution-generating behaviour of firms and individuals is by the use of taxes or charges. (One can also think about subsidies as a "negative" tax or charge.) Indeed, charges appear to be the most popular means of controlling pollution aside from standards. For instance, a 1987 OECD survey of 14 nations found 81 examples of pollution charges in effect (OECD, 1992a). Various examples of environmental charges can be found across all sectors of the economies of most countries.

The transportation sector is particularly interesting from the point of view of charges. Subsidies are frequently used to attract customers from one mode, like private passenger vehicles, to another mode of transportation, like buses, in order to reduce the environmental impact of automobile emissions. Furthermore, a number of countries use differential fuel taxes, like the more favourable rates given diesel fuel in Europe to affect the transportation choices of individuals (OECD, 1992c). Fuel taxes also reduce the number of kilometres driven. It will not be surprising to most people to learn that the United States imposes a lower tax rate on petroleum than do other industrialized countries.

In 1992, for instance, it imposed a tax of about 7 per cent per litre while the comparable tax rate in Japan was 12 per cent and in France was 20 per cent (Callan and Thomas, 1996, p. 139).

Environmental charges are often levied on products that are known to harm the environment. Some jurisdictions in Canada and the United States levy charges on tyres and lead-acid batteries because of the problems associated with their disposal at the end of their useful life. Favourable tax treatments may encourage the recycling of certain materials by, for instance, taxing the use of non-recycled inputs. Recycling technologies are also subsidized in some jurisdictions - either with attractive tax exemptions or up-front subsidies in the initial stages of operation (Tietenberg, 1994, p. 186). Twenty-seven states in the United States provide tax credits, like sales tax exemptions, to encourage the production of recycled products (McClain, 1995). Furthermore, some jurisdictions give tax incentives to promote the transportation of recycled material.

User charges may also be used to reduce the environmental impact of certain activities. These are commonly found in the areas of waste management: charging individual households according to the amount of rubbish needing to be disposed of encourages individuals to generate less waste. Related to these charges is the practice of levying mandatory charges on beverage containers (deposit-refund charges) which has increased their return rate dramatically. Finland, Sweden, Norway and the Netherlands, for instance, have found that well over two thirds of all such containers are returned to the retailer (Callan and Thomas, 1996, p. 149). Roadside waste also seems to have been reduced as a result of this policy. In a similar vein, charges are levied on non-returnable beverage containers in Finland, and on plastic bags in Italy (Turner *et al.*, 1994, p. 162).

Technically speaking, taxing pollution-generating activities gives the incentive to firms (or individuals) to look for other ways of conducting their operations. The closer the tax is tied to the actual pollution itself - a "pure" pollution tax - then the greater the incentive the firm has to reduce the amount it pollutes. Simply put, if the firm is charged for every unit of pollution generated, then it "saves" the tax by investing in cleaner technology.

Taxes or charges are convenient in the sense that they can be applied uniformly across all firms. This feature means that all firms will reduce or abate their pollution until the extra cost of doing so exactly equals the tax (or the extra cost of not abating). As a consequence, all firms, irrespective of how different or heterogeneous they are, will have identical marginal costs of abatement at their chosen levels of production. This result is an attractive feature of charges, and, assuming that the charge is set at the correct level, will lead to the socially acceptable amount of pollution being generated.

Thus, achieving the "acceptable" amount of pollution entails setting tax rates at the correct level. To see what the appropriate tax rate should be from a theoretical perspective, refer back to Figure 2.1 of Chapter 2. The correct tax should be set so that the cost faced by the polluting firm (its marginal private costs of production) coincides with the marginal social costs of production. This tax would then ensure that the firm pays the full cost of its pollution externality. Herein lies one of the difficulties associated with using tax policy to correct for externalities. Often the cost of the externality to the community is rather high. In order to ensure that firms "internalize" this cost, the tax has to be set at an appropriately high level. Politically, this action has proved to be unpopular. As a result, the United States has been very reluctant, with few exceptions, to use pure pollution taxes as such, while Europe has employed them quite extensively, but at rates that are typically too low (Howe, 1994, p. 152; Andersen, 1994). In fact, the goal of taxes in most European countries appears to be revenue generation as opposed to pollution control as such (Andersen, 1994). Imposing a pollution tax that does not cover the actual cost imposed on others of the externality results in firms polluting more than the acceptable quantity. This is one of the big disadvantages with taxes: unless set correctly they may not provide the correct incentive to reduce pollution. Firms may literally continue to pollute as much as they did before the tax, and simply pay the tax as an additional cost of business. Howe (1994, p. 152) reports a Spanish official as saying "we have taxed pollution for twenty years, and industry just pays and goes on polluting".

The consequences of imposing polluting taxes that are too low may be clearly seen in the former Soviet Union. The old system of command and control environmental policies collapsed with the demise of the centrally planned economy. In its place, policies like pollution taxes were implemented. Indeed, since 1 January 1991, a comprehensive system of pollution taxes has been in effect with charges imposed on air pollution from stationary and mobile sources, water pollution and the disposal of solid wastes. Unfortunately, among other things, these taxes were set at too low a level and, to make matters worse, they were not adjusted to take inflation into account. For instance, over the 1992-1994 period while inflation was running at about 300 per cent annually, only a handful of adjustments were made on the tax rates. Not surprisingly, these taxes were not very successful - with the proportion of GNP going to environmental protection expenditures falling over this period, and the amount of emissions rising (Golub and Strukova, 1994).

Germany (i.e., the Federal Republic of Germany prior to re-unification) has relied on a combined system of standards and charges since the early 1970s to control water pollution. In contrast to the experience in the Russian Federation, however, its policy appears to have been quite successful, as the case of the Ruhr River Valley illustrates.

Example 5.2: Water Charges in the Ruhr Valley, Germany

The Ruhr River Valley in Germany provides drinking water for about 5.2 million individuals. Five major reservoirs are located along the Ruhr basin as well as some 100 waste-water treatment plants. Because of its importance to the region, considerable effort has been made by the Ruhr River Association, a public corporation, to improve the quantity and quality of water in the Ruhr catchment.

There are legal requirements for the treatment of municipal wastes. Licences are required in order to discharge waste water, and these licences are only issued if the minimum legal standards are met. In addition to these standards and licences, the German government has imposed a pollution fee or tax for every "pollution unit" discharged into the water. Interestingly, these pollution units are defined over some 11 parameters, depending on the environmental damage associated with the particular effluent. For instance, emissions that use up 50 kilograms of oxygen in the water (i.e., emissions with a biochemical oxygen demand of 50 kilograms of water) constitute one "pollution unit" while three kilograms of phosphorus also constitute a pollution unit (Imhoff, 1995, p. 211). Discharge fees are also imposed.

The system of charges associated with discharging into German waters appears to provide a fairly strong incentive to polluters to find ways of reducing their emissions. The Ruhr River Association has spent a sizeable amount of money, about $U.S. 1.33 billion between 1972 and 1992 for the updating of waste-water treatment plants and storm retention tanks in order to reduce the need to pollute (and hence, reduce the amount of pollution tax to be paid). Water quality in the Ruhr River has improved measurably over the 1972 to 1992 period. For instance, the average BOD in the river at one spot dropped from 53 milligrams per litre to 9 milligrams per litre from 1972 to 1993 (Imhoff, 1995, p. 213). The substantial reduction of various so-called heavy metals (like nickel and cadmium) is directly attributed to the standards and charges levied; and at least two major manufacturing firms went bankrupt because of the discharge fees.

Source: Imhoff (1995); Forsund and Strom (1988, pp. 80-81).

Taxes are typically thought to be superior to standards on a number of fronts. They may be administered rather easily if the jurisdiction relies on the existing tax framework; and, as long as the existing system is effective, then the risk of tax evasion may be considerably lower than the risk of non-compliance with a standard. Note, however, how this attribute of pollution taxes depends critically on the presence of a well-honed taxation system. In the former centrally-planned regimes of Eastern Europe and the former Soviet Union, such a system is unlikely to exist. Hence, pollution taxes in the Russian Federation which necessitate the establishment of a tax-gathering mechanism, may simply not be an effective pollution policy. Another potential advantage of taxes is that they may provide the firm with the incentive to pollute less than it would under a fixed standard. Because taxes impose a cost on firms for every unit of pollution, firms are encouraged to look for pollution-reducing technologies.

However, while taxes have a number of potential advantages over command and control policies, they have one serious drawback. In order to set the correct pollution tax, the policy maker needs to have a significant amount of information: he or she needs to know how much output the firm produces **and**, very importantly, the relationship between this output and pollution. Furthermore, the policy maker needs to know the costs associated with the given pollution - not an easy task for some substances! Information on abatement costs is also essential if the regulator is to know how much pollution will be emitted with the tax. If the regulator is uncertain as to the magnitude of abatement costs, this may have dire consequences for the effectiveness of this measure in terms of the amount of pollution generated. Standards and permits, by contrast, target directly the amount of pollution allowed.

In spite of the difficulties associated with using taxes and charges to curb pollution, their advantages are real. They have the potential to provide a very effective alternative to standards in a number of circumstances.

Legal Liability

One of the least obtrusive public policy responses to environmental degradation is the use of legal liability regimes that encourage firms to internalize the cost of their actions. Legal rules govern virtually every action that we take. If we use our neighbour's property without permission, we can be sued for any damages caused. If a manufacturer produces a defective product, it will be liable for all injuries resulting therefrom. Why not, then, sue a polluter for the damages caused from its emissions?

Before we look at how the legal system may encourage firms to reduce their pollution two important distinctions have to be made. The first distinction is between using legal rules to induce people (firms) to behave in an environmentally desirable way and using legal rules to protect established property rights. Throughout this book we have **assumed** that well-defined property rights are protected by the legal regime. If this were not the case, then bestowing property rights on someone would be meaningless. Therefore, just as ownership of an automobile entitles an individual to legal recourse should it be used without permission, so too does ownership of a pollution right confer some legal rights on its holder. A well-functioning legal system is **fundamental** to the success of property rights. We will now look at how legal rules can directly affect polluter's behaviour rather than indirectly *vis à vis* protecting property rights.

When we talk about legal rules, a second distinction should be kept in mind. Often, legal rules that have been established to protect individuals' rights in some other area can also be employed to protect the environment. These rules are to be contrasted with liability laws that are established solely for the purpose of environmental protection. There are a number of important legal rules that fall into this first category. Riparian or water rights are an important case in point. Although these rights were established primarily to protect individuals' use of water resources for reasonable purposes, they have also been used successfully to curb or eliminate firms from polluting waterways (Brubaker, 1995, chapter 3 and appendix B). Trespass rules have also been used, for instance, to stop others from spraying pesticide on someone else's land, or to control airborne particulate matter arising elsewhere from resting on one's land (Brubaker, 1995, appendices A and C).

There is a good deal of evidence indicating that certain well-established legal principles have been and continue to be successful in curbing some environmentally-damaging behaviour (Brubaker, 1995). Clearly, however, these legal rules have not been enough to control the excesses of the twentieth century - which is why the myriad other approaches to controlling pollution and resource exploitation have been developed over the years. In addition to these established legal rules, the question addressed here is whether we can design laws that are specifically designed to elicit environmentally sound responses from individuals and agents. We turn now to answering this specific question.

Let's consider for a moment the cost to society of a firm's pollution. Suppose that we have one well-defined polluting source (a *point* source) which emits a well-defined substance. The firm can reduce the harm it inflicts on society by installing pollution-abatement equipment, by changing its technology completely to a cleaner one, or by reducing the amount of output it produces. Thus, while taking precaution to reduce pollution entails some costs, it also results in benefits to society. If we were to compare these costs and benefits, we could determine the appropriate amount of precaution that the firm should undertake. This exercise forces us to focus on the fact that firms' actions affect the level of pollution. This appropriate level of precaution results in the "acceptable" level of pollution.

A legal regime could encourage the firm to pollute at this acceptable amount in a number of ways. For the sake of simplicity, we consider two main types of legal liability - negligence and strict liability. Although many other variants of each type of regime exist in reality (Cooter and Ulen, 1988).

Let's begin with a negligence regime. Under legal negligence the firm (or individual) is liable for all of the damages caused by its (his/her) *negligence*. An agent is considered to be negligent if he/she did not take some appropriate level of precaution under the given circumstances. This appropriate level of precaution is typically defined by the courts, which employ, at least in principle, the methodology outlined above. By taking this level of care, the firm is absolved from being liable for any damages that result from its actions. Thus, for instance, one would normally expect **some** pollution to emanate from even the best available technology. As long as the firm is employing the appropriate technology (i.e., the technology that commensurate with taking the appropriate amount of precaution), it will not be compelled to pay the damages arising from its pollution. Should the firm fall short of this standard of precaution, however, then typically it will be liable for **all** of the damages resulting from its pollution. Because it has to pay these damages, the firm is induced to take the appropriate precautions which could lead it to produce an acceptable level of pollution.

Under a negligence rule, as long as the firm is taking the appropriate level of precautions, it is not liable for damages that result from any pollution. In this sense, using a negligence rule does not conform to the desirable polluter pays principle. However, to the extent that the firm is liable for any damages resulting from taking too little precaution, it is strongly encouraged to use clean, environmentally friendly technologies.

A *strict liability* rule is quite different from the negligence rule in one important dimension: the firm is liable for all of the damages caused to others irrespective of whether it employed the appropriate level of precaution or not. Because this means that the firm is facing all of the cost of its pollution, it will still be encouraged to employ the appropriate amount of precaution in its operations. In other words, when faced with strict liability, firms will take precautions to balance the cost of the last "unit" of precaution with its expected liability. Thus, this type of legal regime both induces firms to make appropriate technology choices **and** subjects the firm to the important polluter pays principle.

Before turning to a discussion of the advantages and disadvantages of using legal liability as a means of externalizing pollution costs, let's look at a relatively well-known U.S. example.

Example 5.3: CERCLA and Joint and Several Liability in the United States

In 1980, largely in response to the events in Love Canal, the United States government enacted the *Comprehensive Environmental Response, Compensation, and Liability Act* (CERCLA), also known as the Superfund Act. This act created a $1.6 billion fund that would be used to clean up dangerous hazardous waste sites. (Interestingly, this fund was established mainly from a tax on industrial hazardous-waste generators.) CERCLA imposes so-called *joint and several strict liability* on everyone who has anything to do with the siting and storage of hazardous wastes at these sites.   This includes the producers and transporters of hazardous wastes as well as the owners of the dumps. Joint and several strict liability means that every agent who has had anything at all to do with the production/storing of hazardous wastes is liable for the full costs of any damages that might result from their storage. Technically speaking, all of these firms/individuals are liable to pay up to the full cost of clean-up or any costs stemming from damages to natural resources incurred by the federal or state governments from a hazardous waste site. From a practical perspective, this type of legal rule implies that victims of hazardous waste accidents may sue anyone who has had anything to do with the wastes, irrespective of whether their actions actually caused the accident. As a result of a number of difficulties that arose from this regime, Congress enacted the 1986 *Superfund Amendments Reauthorization Act* (SARA) which gives whoever had to pay the clean-up costs the right to collect from any others who might have contributed to the damages.

Although the CERCLA legislation appears to be rather strict, and thus presumably effective in combating hazardous waste clean-up problems, it has not been as successful as one might have predicted. CERCLA's poor performance has been attributed to a number of practical difficulties that have arisen from its implementation. For instance, the legislation has been interpreted to include everyone who has had anything to do with the hazardous waste in a problematic site **even before** the act was introduced. A case in point is the Hooker Chemical Company which was responsible for the Love Canal fiasco. It was sued under CERCLA even though its actions took place decades before the legislation was enacted. This so-called *retroactive liability* means that firms have found it virtually impossible to insure against the risk of certain types of liability - because the uncertainty is too difficult to measure for the insurance companies. It also means that firms can be sued for damages arising from actions that, at the time, seemed reasonable but now, after the implementation of CERCLA, would lead them open to liability suits.

Because firms are liable, at least in principle, for all of the costs associated with hazardous waste clean-up, they are encouraged by CERCLA legislation to hide their involvement in the process, and to invoke as many delay tactics as the legal system permits to put off paying any damages. These factors have greatly hampered CERCLA's effectiveness. In addition, evidence suggests that the U.S. government had underestimated the magnitude and cost associated with the problem of cleaning up hazardous waste sites. For instance, the average cost of cleaning up a single waste site is about $10 million! Furthermore, the U.S. Environmental Protection Agency has estimated that "about one in four Americans live within four miles of a Superfund toxic waste site and many businesses, particularly small businesses, are ... unfairly burdened..." (Callan and Thomas, 1996, p.569). The legislation basically has the government going in to fund the immediate clean up of these sites, and then it and any victims subsequently sue the appropriate firms or individuals for the resulting damages. So far, only a small fraction of the total clean-up costs has been recovered by the government or victims.   Of the $10 billion or so spent thus far, reportedly only about $4 billion has actually been used to clean-up the sites; legal costs and other transaction costs have soaked up the remainder (Easterbrook, 1995, p. 609).

Sources: Callan and Thomas (1996, chapter 16); Hahn (1988); Davis (1988); Garber (1987); Glass (1988); Easterbrook (1995).

A number of advantages stem from using legal liability rules to encourage firms to pay the cost of their polluting activities. First of all, the reliance of negligence-based rules on the appropriate level of precaution focuses specifically on the trade-off between technology and pollution, which provides a direct incentive for firms to seek out and employ better, cleaner production technologies from the point of view of pollution abatement. The legal regime may also be set to include **all** polluters both in the present and in the future, thus eliminating the need to adjust the policy to apply to, for instance, any new entrant to the industry. Moreover, it may also include polluters across all aspects of economic activity - not just those engaged in some well-defined industry. In this way, the legal regime is an all-encompassing policy instrument. In a similar vein, since individuals themselves may launch legal actions against firms under legal liability rules, some of the burden of monitoring firms' behaviour is shifted from the regulator to individuals. And, since firms know that they are liable for any damages arising from their polluting behaviour and that both the regulator **and** the individual potential victims are monitoring them, they will presumably be induced to pollute only an acceptable amount. Finally, another advantage of legal rules is that the regulator can use a few well-publicized lawsuits as a means of "reminding" firms to take enough precautions. Because firms may be responsible for all damages resulting from their actions, legal rules can provide very strong incentives to behave appropriately (Davis, 1988).

The disadvantages of using legal rules to control polluters are, unfortunately, quite serious. For one thing, when applying legal rules, courts are subject to very strict guidelines. One must be able to show, for instance, that the actions of the firm charged with negligence directly caused the harm in question. In the case of a faulty product, the causality between its use and ensuing harm may not be very difficult to ascertain. In the case of the damages caused by pollution, determining causality in a number of situations may be an extremely difficult if not impossible task. Among other things, one might not be able to prove that it was the emissions of the given firm, for example, that actually caused a respiratory illness, or, that the illness itself was categorically caused by the pollutant of this firm. Furthermore, certain illnesses are latent and come to light long after the polluting firm is out of business. Moreover, examples abound of firms declaring bankruptcy after facing multiple suits for damages caused by their emissions. In the United States, Johns-Manville, the owner of several asbestos plants, declared bankruptcy after over $U.S 2 billion of lawsuits were lodged against it (Dewees, 1992a). The Union Carbide plant in Bhopal India, after a leak of methyl isocyanide killed thousands of people in 1984, did likewise.

Another problem with legal rules as a means of controlling pollution arises from the fact that often relatively low costs are imposed on a large number. It becomes, therefore, not worthwhile for any one of the 'victims' to litigate. This problem has been reduced in the United States with the use of *class-action suits* - whereby all victims can band together and launch one collective suit. However, if the exposure to the pollutant were different across the victims leading to different types of injuries, class-action suits will not work. It is also costly to identify all of the members of the class. On a related matter, the costs associated with using the legal system are enormous. One extensive study into the matter found that victims of asbestos received only about 37 per cent of the compensation paid out once account was taken of litigation costs (Dewees, 1992a, p. 25). Using the legal system is an expensive way of encouraging good behaviour by polluters. Davis (1988, p. 505) reports of one study of the Love Canal disaster which estimates that it would have cost about $4 million to have avoided the problem, about $125 million to clean up the site, while it ended up costing some $2.5 **billion** in compensation through the courts.

As with all measures of controlling environmental degradation, the use of legal liability rules has advantages and disadvantages. Relying on liability rules seems particularly useful when the number of victims and injurers is small, rendering it a fairly straightforward matter for the victims to take the injurers to court to settle their dispute. Brubaker (1995) and Dewees (1992a, 1992b) provide ample evidence of the successful use of legal rules in this regard. However, when large numbers of victims or injurers are implicated in an environmental action, the legal system may not be the best means of solving the problem and encouraging the most appropriate use of environmental resources.

International Agreements

Another way of encouraging countries to deal with environmental problems has been the use of international agreements. Although difficult to enforce in any court of law, these agreements have been used with increasing frequency over the past decade or so and appear to work mostly with the help of peer pressure.

That is to say that the international community brings pressure to bear on those countries that signed an agreement to "encourage" them to honour the agreement. In addition, international agreements tend to command a great deal of media attention. Consequently, pressures from within the signatory countries themselves may also encourage them to meet the various commitments.

Some of the more notable international agreements include the *United Nations Framework Convention on Climate Change* of 1994; *United Nations Conference on Environment and Development (UNCED)* - more commonly referred to as the Rio Summit - held in Rio de Janeiro in 1992; the *Montreal Protocol* of 1987; and the *London Dumping Convention* of 1972. The Convention on Climate Change which came into force in March 1994 commits developed countries to control greenhouse gas emissions so as to reduce the chances of global warming. The Rio Summit resulted in the release of a number of internationally-agreed-upon documents: *Agenda 21* outlines a voluntary plan towards sustainable development for the new millennium; the *Rio Declaration* outlines a number of principles, including the polluter pays principle, that should guide countries in their environmental and development policies; the *Statement of Forest Principles* outlines the need for international cooperation in the management of forests; and the *Convention on Biodiversity* which, among other things, is designed to find measures to counteract species extinction. The Montreal Protocol is designed to phase out the use of ozone-depleting substances, while the London Dumping Convention arose from a desire to limit the dumping of wastes at sea. The dumping of certain substances is banned completely, while the dumping of other substances is subject to some control.

Example 5.4: The United Nations Framework Convention on Climate Change

The earth naturally produces a certain amount of greenhouse gases which, when mixed with the naturally occurring terrestrial radiation, will heat up the lower atmosphere thus keeping the surface of the earth at a life-supporting temperature. Over the past hundreds of years, and especially since the industrial revolution, the production of greenhouse gases has increased tremendously. These include carbon dioxide which results from the burning of fossil fuels, like coal and oil, as well as the burning of forests; methane arising from modern farming practices as well as from coal mining and natural gas production; nitrous oxide from fertilizers and chemical production; and chlorofluorocarbons which are widely used in refrigerators and air conditioners. As the concentration of greenhouse gases increases, the amount of terrestrial radiation trapped in the lower atmosphere also increases thus enhancing the natural greenhouse effect. The Intergovernmental Panel on Climate Change projects that if the pattern of greenhouse gas accumulation continues, average surface temperatures could rise by two to three degrees Celsius over the next 100 years. Because the impact of the greenhouse effect is global in nature, international cooperation is essential to control this environmental problem.

Over 150 governments signed the Convention on Climate Change at the Rio Earth Summit of 1992, which came into effect on 21 March 1994.   These countries agreed to establish measures to reduce greenhouse gas emissions. An interesting feature of this agreement is that it explicitly recognizes the different priorities of poorer and richer countries regarding global-warming issues. Richer nations have agreed to help the developing countries, both financially and technically, to put policies into effect that would reduce their greenhouse gas emissions over time. The developed nations that signed the agreement, called Annex I countries, have also agreed to reduce their emissions of carbon dioxide and other greenhouse gases to 1990 levels by the year 2000. Unfortunately, the most recent estimates suggest that the target set for Annex I countries will not be met while emissions from non Annex I countries is expected to be almost 60 per cent higher in 2000 than in 1990.

Source: U.N. press releases PR3-94, PR8-94, PR3-95, available from www.unep.ch/iucc/prx-9x; and Global Climate Change Information Programme fact sheets: www.doc.mmu.ac.uk/aric/fccc.html;   OECD (1993); Brown *et al.* (1997).

In addition to these international agreements whose express purpose is to address some environmental issue, numerous other types of agreements have touched upon various environmental concerns while treating other issues. The recent North American Free Trade Agreement (NAFTA) is an interesting case in point.

Before leaving the topic of international agreements, it needs to be stressed that these agreements are only as effective as the policies that implement their provisions in each country. The process of reaching a consensus within and between countries over environmental concerns is extremely complicated and murky. Many interest groups exist on both sides of environmental issues, with the final policies typically reflecting these diverse and conflicting interests. That we actually come to some agreement over some of these issues is truly remarkable!

Further, even the more successful agreements, like the Montreal Protocol designed to arrest the use of ozone-depleting substances, may be hampered by the actions of recalcitrant and non-signatory nations. Indeed, the fact that CFC production has been drastically reduced since 1987 has given rise to a flourishing black market in this substance. According to officials in Miami, for instance, "CFCs are the port's second most profitable contraband after drugs" (*The Economist*, 9 December 1995, p. 63). CFC production is also rising rather dramatically in developing countries. Once again, the tension between developing and developed countries comes to the fore in the environmental arena.

Combining Environmental Policies

Thus far, our discussion of the various approaches to controlling the environment has treated each policy independently of each other. In reality, we rarely find only one policy in place for any given environmental programme - they are usually used in conjunction with each other resulting in a richer, more effective overall approach to controlling environmental degradation.

For some time now it has been recognized that combining standards and charges would result in an environmental policy that would achieve the objective of pollution reduction while alleviating some of the problems associated with standards. For instance, charging a fee per unit of any pollution that exceeds the set standard would encourage firms to meet the standard while providing them with a sort of "pressure valve" that would permit them to exceed the standard if circumstances warrant it (Spence and Weitzman, 1993). In addition to providing firms with a much needed cushion for their activities, firms would also be encouraged to seek out cleaner technologies. Coupling taxes and standards would also result in firms paying at least some of the costs of their pollution - conforming to the desirable polluter pays principle.

Rather than combining standards and charges, Andersen (1994) suggests that charges and subsidies should be used jointly. After an extensive review of the European experiences with pollution taxes, Andersen concludes that taxes and subsidies would constitute an effective policy mix. To encourage firms to pollute at the "acceptable" level, a substantial pollution tax would have to be levied - a tax that would be politically difficult to impose. However, charging a lower tax and then subsidizing pollution abatement may result in the same desirable level of pollution but may be more palatable to firms and politicians.

Tradeable property rights schemes are often implemented on top of command and control policies. The Southern Californian RECLAIM programme was established specifically as a means of meeting U.S. Federal air-quality standards. One of the few restrictions on trading in the U.S. sulphur dioxide trading programme is that air-quality standards continue to be met in each state. Halon production in the United States is limited by a standard and taxed. One can show that putting a policy of tradeable permits together with taxes is an effective way of setting an absolute limit on the amount of pollution emitted while generating much-needed revenue for the government (Grafton and Devlin, 1996). Typically such a policy has yet to be established. However, as tradeable property rights become more common, cash-strapped governments will likely become interested in implementing schemes that will generate revenue as well as effectively control pollution.

International agreements essentially set the "standard" to which signatory countries agree to adhere. As such, other policies, such as the ones mentioned here, have to be implemented in each country in order to put into effect the international agreement. The Montreal Protocol gave rise to tradeable permit schemes, taxes and standards, while the Convention on Biodiversity has resulted in increased incentives to identify new species and research the commercial value of known species (Callan and Thomas, 1996, p. 23). Legal liability rules are usually articulated around a regulated standard. Hazardous waste producers in the United States are subject to both a tax on the quantity of waste generated as well as the threat of legal liability if these wastes are stored inappropriately.

Before ending this subsection, it is worthwhile to say a few words about another type of policy - environmental bonds - that could easily be used in conjunction with other environmental measures. Firms or individuals with the potential to harm the environment could be asked by the regulatory authority to post a bond which would be used to pay for any environmental harm that might occur even though standards are being met. Thus, for instance, a bond could be posted by a carrier transporting hazardous waste that otherwise conformed to environmental standards, with the cash value of the bond being used to cover the environmental costs of any spillage While some research has been done on the theoretical advantages of environmental bonds, they have rarely been used as an environmental policy measure for a variety of reasons (Perrings, 1989; Hanley *et al.*, 1997, chapter 3). For instance, the value of the bond is supposed to be set high enough so that it can compensate for damages should they occur, but this may erect a barrier such that small but "clean" firms are discouraged from entering into a particular activity. Nevertheless, bonds do encourage firms and individuals to monitor their polluting activities and may well play a greater role in future environmental management strategies.

As individuals and governments become increasingly aware of the importance of the environment and natural resources, and as measures of environmental degradation become more available, policy makers worldwide are subject to mounting pressure to implement appropriate policies. In addition to the traditional command and control approach to solving the problem of externalities, more and more emphasis is being placed on other, more decentralized, measures that rely increasingly on providing firms and individuals with the incentive to make socially-desirable - albeit self-interested - decisions. A sensible approach to environmental policy is one which mixes various policies in order to gain the advantages of different approaches while mitigating their disadvantages.

5.2   POVERTY AND THE ENVIRONMENT

A discussion of the various ways of dealing with environmental problems would be incomplete if it did not at least mention the importance of population and poverty in attenuating these problems. Indeed, even the Convention on Climate Change explicitly recognized that developing countries have special needs and should be treated differently in comparison to the wealthy western world.

Some evidence suggests a negative relationship exists between income and air pollution: in other words, as income increases on average so too does the quality of air (World Bank, 1992). However, it is important to note that this relationship does not always work in the same direction. Some have suggested that environmental degradation actually worsens as economies begin to grow out of poverty, then, once a certain level of wealth is attained, the opposite relationship is observed (Stern *et al.*, 1996). If this pattern holds true, then policies geared towards improving the economic circumstances of poor countries will not necessarily attenuate their environmental problems - at least not immediately.

For a variety of reasons, poor countries are also ones that are most prone to burgeoning populations. Population growth in areas where the basic essentials of life are in short supply and where poverty is the norm leads individuals to take **any** available measure to obtain basic sustenance. Population growth in wealthy countries, however, does not pose the same kind of difficulties - the United States, for instance, has experienced tremendous population growth over the past century, yet the state of its environment is arguably better today than it was, say, 20 years ago. Thus, it is not population growth, *per se*, that results in environmental degradation; rather, it is population growth coupled with poverty that places tremendous strains of the environment. Part of the debate, however, centres on whether population growth causes poverty or whether poverty causes population growth. Much has been written on this issue (Dasgupta, 1995). It is clear that environmental policy must be sensitive to the economic circumstances of the population. In this sense, international cooperation becomes crucial if poorer countries are to arrest the environmental degradation occurring within their borders.

The impact of poverty on the environment and resources can be clearly illustrated by the situation in the Brazilian rainforest. There, people are forced to use ineffective slash and burn techniques to eke out a temporary means of survival. These poor Brazilians do not care that the systematic burning of the rainforest is increasing the level of carbon dioxide in the earth's atmosphere. Nor are they worried about the fact that the destruction of many species of plants means that future pharmaceuticals are in jeopardy. Why not? Because these people are trying to find a way of obtaining enough food each day to survive. A population that has to worry about basic human needs will not and, indeed, should not worry about long-term environmental problems and future generations.

The Brazilian rainforest situation has received world attention precisely because its destruction imposes a global externality. The Convention on Biological Diversity with its explicit recognition of the special problems associated with developing countries reflects the global community's concern with the rainforest. However, for more local problems, like, for instance, the air quality situation in Mexico City, finding an acceptable solution is more problematic. Combating environmental degradation in areas where basic necessities are scarce means first of all that the problems associated with the procurement of these basic essentials should be solved. This problem is a perennial one and has been treated extensively in the rich and vast literature on development economics. We believe that individuals should be given the tools and know-how in order to become self-reliant and to develop in a sustainable way. Until developing countries are able to alleviate the problems of poverty, their citizens will not be able to partake fully in activities designed to stop environmental degradation.

Imposing environmental standards in many developing countries is also difficult. Regulations that stipulate penalties for non-compliance are hard to monitor when the polluters are numerous small-scale operators. Regulation also presumes some sort of devolution of power - where the "regulator" is entrusted with the task of monitoring and enforcing the standards. Most developing countries have extremely centralized governments. In some of these countries, bribery and corruption are important forces with which to reckon. Although by no means unique to the developing world, officials may look upon bribes as a means of supplementing their meagre wages (OECD, 1992a).

In cases where populations are fighting for survival, no type of private property-right regime will solve the environmental problem. Poor Brazilians will continue to use any method possible to acquire land to feed their families. Private ownership of the rainforest is unlikely to stop this from happening because the future means very little to people who do not know if they are going to eat in any given day. National and international environmental policy must, therefore, acknowledge and deal with the problems associated with poverty in order to address adequately the costs of environmental degradation.

5.3   GREEN ACCOUNTS

Although so-called green accounts do not constitute an environmental policy *per se*, their establishment may help facilitate the setting of policy targets and hence they merit a brief discussion. Green accounts refer to an accounting system that takes explicit account of the stock of environmental amenities in a particular country or region. Virtually every country has a system of national accounts that tracks an economy's national income and wealth. To facilitate inter-country comparison, these accounts are usually structured in a common well-defined way. Typically these accounts do not take into consideration the natural resources of the country or its stock of, say, clean air or water. While the accounts consider the depreciation of human-made capital, they completely ignore natural capital. Some have argued that since the national accounts are trying to measure the well-being of a country then they should take account of its natural resources and environment. In fact, efforts have been focused on introducing natural capital and the environment into national accounts since the early 1970s (Tinbergen and Hueting, 1992).

A number of proposals have been put forth regarding how countries might take account of natural capital and environmental amenities, taking into account the problems associated with trying to put a value on these resources. For instance, Daly and Cobb (1994) devote a considerable amount of space to discussing their proposed *Index of Sustainable Economic Welfare*. This index takes account of certain factors that are ignored in the traditional national accounts, like income inequality, improvements in health, as well as various measures of the cost of environmental degradation and resource depletion. While this index is well thought out and takes account of most of the salient factors, it does not resolve the disagreements associated with how to measure many of the factors. Unfortunately, it is largely these disagreements that have hindered the development of a standard green accounting system.

At the moment, national accounts only measure market transactions. All non-market transactions wherein "prices" are not readily available - like household production and volunteer work - are excluded from its measure. One attempt to take account of these non-market transactions as well as the cost of divorce and crime, resource depletion and pollution, suggests that the economic well-being of residents of the United States has fallen on a per capita basis since about 1970 (Redefining Progress, 1995). However, since the values placed on many non-market transactions are open to interpretation, one must always look upon such estimates with some degree of healthy scepticism.

In spite of the difficulties associated with taking account of our natural resources and their use, a great deal of work is being done on determining how to introduce the stock of resources and environmental degradation into a system of national accounts. Doing so certainly makes sense from a number of points of view. For instance, when making inter-country comparisons concerning the well-being of inhabitants it would be very useful to know something about the natural capital of each country. It would also be extremely useful to know how this natural capital is being used - its rate of depreciation. As we mentioned in the introduction of this book, using natural capital at an inappropriately fast rate could, and has, led to the devastation of whole communities. Green accounts would also facilitate the evaluation of a country's environmental policies. Rather than taking the piece-meal approach to policy evaluation as is the current norm, having a measure of national environmental attributes would allow us to see how each country is doing on aggregate from an environmental policy perspective.

5.4 ENVIRONMENTAL DEGRADATION, NOW WHAT?

Society has a number of ways of improving the environmental health of an economy. Which policy to pursue, however, depends critically on a number of factors, typically focusing on the nature of the externality itself. Is the pollution stemming from a point or non-point source? How many sources are involved in its production? Is the externality local, national or global in nature? And so on. Standards are best used when the number of polluting sources is small and their costs of abatement are similar, and when monitoring is easy. They are also very useful when the amount of pollution has a critical impact on the environment. For instance, very small amounts of CFCs can have a detrimental impact on the ozone layer. Whenever it is important to control precisely the emissions of a pollutant, standards may be the appropriate policy.

Taxes and charges, if set properly, not only reduce the amount of pollution emitted, but also generate revenue to help defray the costs of environmental degradation. However, they are often set at too low a level resulting in the discharge of an unacceptably high level of emissions. Aside from revenue generation, which is an important consideration for today's fiscally-restrained governments, taxes provide an economic incentive for firms to try to reduce the amount of pollution generated.

The goals of the policy maker also affect the type of environmental policy pursued. One of the reasons why pollution taxes have typically been set too low is because of the political clout wielded by certain industries. Political considerations have also influenced the monitoring and setting of standards, such as in the pulp and paper industry in Canada, as well as the siting of hazardous wastes (Nadis, 1996). Policy makers have to balance the well-being of current and future populations with certain pragmatic considerations like winning votes and how to cope with the ensuing unemployment should an important, but dirty, plant shut down in their jurisdiction. While outside the mandate of this book, it is important to note that political considerations play a significant role in the actual design of environmental policy.

5.5 FURTHER READING

A number of excellent environmental texts provide superb reviews of the various approaches to environmental degradation - including Tietenberg (1994), Turner et al. (1994), Hodge (1995b), Callan and Thomas (1996). Tietenberg and Callan and Thomas provide many excellent "real-world" examples of various policies mostly in the United States; Turner *et al.* and Hodge provide more European examples. Further Euro-centred analyses are contained in various papers in Klaassen and Forsund (1994); these papers are quite accessible to the non-economist. The OECD has a number of very useful and easy-to-read documents describing the movement since the early 1980s towards the use of decentralized policies to control the environment (OECD, 1980, 1991, 1992a, 1992c and 1993). The politics associated with reaching international consensus is nicely described in OECD (1992b). Brubacker (1995) provides an excellent discussion on how property rights facilitate legal recourse for environmental damages. A useful discussion of the pros and cons of using legal rules to internalize externalities is provided in a straightforward manner by Dewees (1992b).

An excellent, although dense, synthesis of issues associated with population, poverty and the environment, is contained in Dasgupta (1995) - which also provides an outstanding bibliography for the interested reader. Daly and Cobb's (1994) book covers an extraordinary number of topics in the area of sustainable development. They do a particularly fine job at discussing the various factors that ought to be taken into account when establishing green accounts. However, they do not adequately address the problems associated with green accounting. Jacobs (1991) and Tinbergen and Hueting (1992) present useful discussions on the need for green accounts.

6

Property Rights for the Common Good

6.1   LESSONS LEARNED

Economics and the Environment

For some, the word "economics" conjures up images of environmental degradation by big business, unbridled greed, resource exploitation - in short, visions that are anathema to a caring, environmentally sensitive society. In fact, economics has much to offer people who are concerned about environmental degradation and resource exploitation, and provides guidance as to how these difficult problems may be solved.

The "economics" approach to the environment, including natural resources, focuses on the importance of identifying the *externality* that underlies the problem at hand. Environmental problems stem from the fact that the full cost of someone's actions is not being borne by that person (or firm). Polluters do not pay the full cost of their emissions, and resource users do not take into account the costs imposed on others by their activities. Once the externality is identified, we need to determine who is not paying the full cost of their actions. Solving the problem entails forcing the polluter or the user to *internalize* this external cost. The essence of the economic model, therefore, is that everyone should be forced to bear all of the costs of their actions.

To illustrate the power of the economics framework - and why some polluters would prefer that environmentalists did not rely on it - let's consider the example of the *Exxon Valdez* oil spill off the coast of Alaska. On 24 March

1989, the *Exxon Valdez* oil tanker ran into a reef and spewed some 45 million litres (11 million gallons) of crude oil into Prince William Sound - rendering it the biggest oil spill in U.S. waters (Carson *et al.*, 1994, p .1).   The state of Alaska sued the owner of the tanker for damages.   When trying to determine the extent of the damages, the state of Alaska employed a state-of-the-art economics technique to put a dollar value on the *existence* value of the natural resource (clean Prince William Sound water).   The technique used was a *contingent valuation survey* which was designed to elicit how much individuals from across the United States valued this resource.   Two points need to be emphasized here.   First of all, the fact that explicit account was taken of the value accruing to a resource because of its existence represents a major step forward to environmental economists who have been touting the importance of existence value for years (Hanley, 1989; Johansson, 1990; Bishop *et al.*, 1995). And, secondly, the use of a contingent valuation survey to try to quantify the value of Prince William Sound represents an important step in the process of implementing the economics approach to managing the environment.   Although a broad range of estimates was established for the existence value of Prince William Sound - from about 3 billion dollars to 9 billion dollars - they provided much-needed guidance for the subsequent legal suit.

By considering the notion of an externality, the economics model allows us to analyse the problems of pollution as well as of inappropriate resource management.   We could also look at the question in a slightly different way. If we were to determine all of the benefits associated with a particular activity - say, pulp and paper processing - and all of the costs associated with the activity, **including** any externalities, we could determine the socially desirable level of this activity as well as the "acceptable" amount of pollution arising from it. Either way of looking at the problem of externalities leads us to the same conclusion: all benefits and costs have to be taken into account in order that society be assured of a safe, clean environment, and appropriately managed natural resources.   Sounds simple?   As a number of cases have demonstrated over the course of this book, taking into account all the costs and benefits arising from any given activity is rarely straightforward.

Let's consider the first task to be undertaken - the identification of the relevant externality.   A pulp and paper mill that is discharging chlorinated waste into a river is fairly easy to identify.   The externality is the increased biochemical oxygen demand in the water and the attendant costs associated with the loss of fish and plants.   However, what about identifying the externality associated with a large body of water into which hundreds of firms are emitting?   The dumping of wastes in the oceans presents one example where the identification of the culprits is an extremely difficult task; identifying the contributors to acid rain poses a similar problem. And, as fishing in the high seas clearly illustrates, determining who is over using a common-pool resource amounts to a formidable task.

Once the actual externality is determined, the next step is to look at whether or not the activity that generated the externality should be undertaken. In other words, do the benefits associated with the activity justify all of its costs? Some activities should cease once costs and benefits are taken into account: slashing and burning the Amazon rainforest may be questioned from an economic standpoint; the continued use of chlorofluorocarbons is socially undesirable; and so on. Other activities should continue but - and this but is crucial - policies have to be put in place in order to ensure that only an "acceptable" amount of the externality is imposed on society.

Because the economics framework takes explicit account of costs and benefits, it implies that a policy of zero-pollution is sensible only under very particular circumstances. It also implies that economic growth is not necessarily a bad thing. In fact, economic growth is good for society provided it takes place within the context of well-formulated, effective environmental policies. Environmental policies may be set to accommodate this growth. Consider, for instance, the RECLAIM programme underway in southern California. New firms are able to enter the Los Angeles market even though they may be contributing to air pollution - provided that they purchase sufficient "emission reduction credits" from existing firms. Allowing such growth encourages firms with better, cleaner technologies to enter and remain in the market while inducing dirtier ones to leave it.

It is interesting to note that environmental degradation does not necessarily increase with wealth. As we noted in Chapter 5, as countries become wealthier air quality may actually increase (World Bank, 1992). Thus, to the extent that balanced economic growth leads to increased incomes within a country, then, at some point we would expect a stronger demand for better environmental conditions. Furthermore, countries with the highest incomes also have the lowest rates of population growth (World Bank, 1992) - again reducing the pressure on natural resources and the environment.

Technological change, one of the byproducts of economic growth, may also advance environmentalists' causes. Although some have suggested that technological advances are at the root of our current environmental difficulties, this view ignores the fact that individuals respond to incentives (Kaufman, 1994, chapter 9). Rather than "blaming" technology for environmental degradation, we should be thinking about how technology may further the cleaning up of our environment. Consider, for instance, the spectacular changes that have been made in fuel efficiency, sparked by increasing costs, over the past decade or more: the Boeing 757 and Airbus 320 use 30 per cent less fuel in 1995 than ten years previously. In the mid 1960s about 75 kilograms of metal were required to manufacture 1,000 soda-pop cans, by 1995 only about 20 per cent of this amount was required (Easterbrook, 1995, p. 258). Zero economic growth dampens the incentive for research and development into more productive, cleaner, safer technologies.

The Importance of Information

In determining the acceptable amount of pollution to generate it is necessary to calculate the costs associated with the externality. As you can well imagine, this is an extremely difficult task. Nevertheless, the ability of the regulator to promote the "appropriate" amount of the externality hinges on having enough information to determine this acceptable level. It cannot be overemphasized that the informational requirements underlying this process are immense. Determining the impact of something as ordinary as, say, sulphur dioxide emissions is extremely complex. First, one has to identify all of the effects of this emission - on air quality, on acid rain, and so on. Then, one has to determine the costs associated with each effect. Consider, for instance, the cost to society of poor air quality alone. It will depend upon the geophysical characteristics of the affected areas, like altitude, air currents and the natural acidity of soils and rocks, as well on as population density and the extent of other pollutants. Factors like the state of health of the affected population also play an important role.

Compounding the many problems associated with determining the costs imposed on the **present** population from the pollution or mismanagement of resources is the fact that **future** generations are also affected. How does the policy maker determine the costs to future generations of, say, the extinction of a species in the rainforest? What about the costs of global warming to our children and grandchildren?

Just because information is difficult to obtain does not mean to say that its pursuit is not worthwhile. On the contrary, the payoff to policy makers from having even some information can be enormous. For instance, although researchers do not know precisely the impact on humans of ozone-layer thinning, they do know that it may lead to serious health consequences. The international community has thus cooperated to establish stringent standards for the emissions of ozone-depleting substances to which each signatory country is bound to adhere. The fact that researchers cannot determine with certainty the exact costs of the ozone-layer depletion has not prevented policy makers from taking a stance based on limited information. The same may be said for greenhouse gases, acid rain, and various other externalities of which the exact impact may be unknown but which require, nevertheless, policy prescriptions to reduce their external effects.

One response to the need for additional information in order to evaluate the full costs and benefits associated with economic activities has been the growing use of environmental assessments, as endorsed by Principle 17 of the declaration by the United Nations Conference on Environment and Development (Sadler, 1994, p. 3). The number of countries using environmental impact assessments has grown considerably since the late 1960s. Their purpose is straightforward: to provide policy makers with information on the current and future impact of any given project. Environmental assessments are typically conducted for publicly-funded projects. However, as government money often backs large private projects, these too may be subject to scrutiny (www.cec.org/english/database/law/us/07/07-02.htm). In many respects, an environmental assessment is trying to do what the economics framework has been advocating for years - namely, trying to ascertain all of the costs and benefits associated with a given project. One measure of the growing recognition of the importance of environmental assessments is the fact that since 1994 the World Bank has required such an assessment before funding relevant projects (Goodland and Edmundson, 1994, p. vii).

Agreement is widespread on the importance of information for the framing of policy responses. The fact that information itself has many of the characteristics of a *public good* - once information is in the public domain, one cannot exclude anyone from using it, and its use by any one person does not affect anyone else's use of the information - has meant that private agencies will under invest in the gathering of information. However, this shortfall is being made up by the efforts of numerous government agencies world wide that are investing in information on the impact of certain pollutants in the environment. A good example of multilateral cooperation is the Inter-governmental Panel on Climate Change (IPCC) which entails thousands of researchers and scientists from around the world examining the potential problems that may arise from the emissions of greenhouse gases. The widespread availability of computers has eased the gathering and analyses of data, improving the situation tremendously. A relatively recent phenomenon, the World Wide Web, has also improved significantly the dissemination of important and timely information to researchers and decision-makers.

Property Rights versus Alternative Solutions

Creating tradeable property rights internalizes the externality problem by forcing individual agents to consider the costs of their actions on others. Let's consider first the case of pollution. Establishing a tradeable property right over the pollutant itself implies that every unit of pollution **costs** the firm the price of the right. This statement is true even if the firm does not actually "buy" the rights because each right it owns has an *opportunity cost* - the price that it could fetch on the market. As long as the policy maker establishes the appropriate number of rights on the market, the price of the right will reflect social costs and hence the externality associated with a unit of pollution will be internalized (i.e., paid by the firm). We have provided numerous examples of tradeable property rights to deal with pollution, and it has become clear that how these rights are implemented affects critically their ability to solve the problem. In general, an "ideal" property right would embrace six characteristics - exclusivity, flexibility, divisibility, transferability, duration and quality of title, although, as we analysed various property-right schemes in this book, we were led to the conclusion that the last two characteristics - namely duration and quality of title - are not so important in the context of property rights created to solve the externality problem. Using a stylized schema of these property right characteristics allows us to determine what an effective property-right system would look like and, to a large extent, when such a system is likely to be a suitable policy. For instance, if it is possible to identify something over which the right is defined - a unit of pollution - then the policy is likely to be suitable. If transfers cannot easily take place across polluters, then such a policy will not work.

Property rights are also an effective way of managing natural resources. Community rights have successfully been used to manage irrigation projects, some coastal fisheries, forests and grazing land. Community rights seem to work best when the resource in question has well-defined geographical boundaries and when the community is effective at both controlling exploitation by outsiders and its own members. Private property rights are a relatively recent innovation for renewable common-pool resources and have been applied in a number of fisheries in Canada, the United States, New Zealand, Australia and Iceland. Provided that the costs of exclusion are low relative to the potential benefits, private rights can bring significant benefits to both the resource and resource users. Many examples also exist of a mix of property rights. For instance, the conservation of biodiversity in a number of countries involves state, private and community rights. Where natural resources are well managed, property rights provide an appropriate set of incentives and penalties so that individuals consider the effect of their actions on the resource and other users.

One interesting feature of the property-right solution, as opposed to government imposed standards, is that it is a *decentralized* solution. The relevant agents decide amongst themselves how much pollution to emit, how many fish to harvest, or how many trees to fell, given the constraint that a right is required for each unit of pollution, fish, or whatever. In many cases, the decentralized solution is desirable because it encourages each agent to make self-interested decisions while respecting the overall constraint determined by the number of rights on the market.

Clearly, the property-right solution is not the only way to deal with externalities. We have discussed at length other ways of controlling externalities: standards, taxes, legal liability rules, environmental bonds, and international agreements. Taxes and legal liability rules are also decentralized solutions. The major drawback with taxes stems from the fact that if the tax rate is set too low - and it typically is - then firms will continue to pollute too much. Taxes that are too low do not provide enough of an incentive for firms or resource users to reduce their externalilites. The property-right solution does not suffer from this drawback since it targets directly the level of the externality (or the activity which generates the externality). However, taxes do provide governments with much-needed revenue with which to undertake, for instance, important environmental projects. One way to reconcile these two approaches is to implement a tradeable permit scheme and then tax back the economic rents or profits that accrue to the property right (Grafton and Devlin, 1996). Liability rules, while having the potential to provide the incentive to reduce externalities, are not easy to implement in practice and hence are typically not recommended as a general rule. Environmental bonds are useful but are limited to situations where the actions of firms can be well observed and may impose significant liquidity constraints on businesses. Finally, international agreements provide a mechanism that encourages individual countries to establish some type of environmental policy to target the agreed-upon problem. Without these agreements, some international environmental problems will simply not be resolved.

Standards, or a command and control type policy, are used virtually everywhere and represent a centralized solution to externalities. Their biggest limitation arises from the fact that they typically treat everyone the same. Thus, for instance, firms do not usually have the option of polluting more than the standard, nor are they encouraged to pollute below the standard to gain some savings. Treating different firms identically is not a cost-effective way of reducing pollution. In spite of their limitations, standards hold a particular appeal to policy makers. Standards may be used by the government to represent a tangible action geared towards solving an externality problem. Governments, therefore, by establishing standards, are seen to be "doing something". An interesting feature of the policy landscape in most countries is the blending of standards with other, more decentralized, policies.

6.2   THE IMPORTANCE OF INCENTIVES

One theme that has emerged throughout this book is the importance of incentives when trying to solve the problems of externalities. Policies may induce people to make decisions that are "in their best interest", or they may force people to make decisions in spite of their best interest. It should be clear by now that policies that fit in this first category have a much better chance of being successful than ones that fight against self-interested behaviour. Regulating fishing catches by imposing length restrictions on boats leads fishers to use broader boats with more sophisticated equipment - negating any positive effect of the length restriction. By contrast, giving fishers transferable property rights over any given species of fish is a much more effective policy as fishers have the incentive to "look after" their right. Giving people a choice of how to meet some objective, rather than compelling them to meet the objective by behaving in a certain way, has proved to be a successful strategy.

While governments through their choice of policies may provide the incentive to firms to behave in a socially acceptable fashion, they are not the only source of encouragement. Consumers are having a tremendous impact on the decisions of firms in the environmental **and** resource management arena. "Green" consumerism is altering fundamentally the way in which firms conduct their businesses. In fact, some might even argue that the impetus coming from consumer demand is far stronger than any government policies have been in terms of leading the way for change. Consider the various ways in which consumers have shaped the array of products we now have before us. In the United States in the early 1970s, the environmental group Friends of the Earth ran a successful campaign to encourage Schweppes to use returnable bottles; Marks & Spencer, a British retail chain, made a point of indicating that their meat had not grazed on rainforest pasture during the heyday of deforestation in 1989; the Swiss retailer Migros has a computer programme that determines the "eco-balance" of its packaging; Loblaws, a Canadian grocery chain, was the first large grocery outlet in Canada to launch an incredibly successful "green" line of products (*The Economist*, September 1990, Survey). Who could forget the cute little seal pup pictured with Brigitte Bardot that spearheaded a campaign against the clubbing of seals? Fur producers have seen their market decimated because of green consumerism and have been forced to change their practices for killing animals. And the list goes on. The impact of consumer demand on greening products, reducing packaging, minimizing chemical additives and the like is truly staggering.

The fact that green consumers are wielding an enormous amount of power is not without its problems, particularly when consumers' opinions are formed on the basis of false or mis-information. Consider the case of the apple pesticide *Alar*. In 1989 an episode of the U.S. current-affairs television programme "60 Minutes" aired an alarming broadcast in which it was indicated that the pesticide Alar threatened the health of children. As a result, the pesticide was banned as a "probable" carcinogen by the Environmental Protection Agency. It is now known that this "scare" was largely unfounded. The reaction of the public to the "60 Minutes" programme was quick - quite naturally. The reaction of the U.S. EPA was also rather quick, leading one to speculate as to whether its reaction was based on scientific knowledge or, rather, on the reaction of the general public (Easterbrook, 1995).

Another downfall of this green consumer movement is the ability of businesses to use clever marketing tools to "fool" consumers. The mere fact that a product is labelled a "green" product does not make it so. Some businesses are taking advantage of this movement to encourage uninformed consumers to purchase their goods. "Green" marketing has become a multi-million dollar business.

6.3   THE IMPORTANCE OF INSTITUTIONS

Any policy that is implemented in an "unsuitable" milieu is doomed to failure. To be successful, a policy must be implemented in an environment in which rules and codes of behaviour conducive to that policy exist. To see the importance of a suitable institutional framework, consider the problems associated with implementing environmental policy in the former Soviet Union. In the communist era, managers were rewarded on the basis of achieving a given production quota, and virtually no firm had the incentive to comply with environmental standards. Even the central government which "owned" the various natural resources was not induced to promulgate and enforce environmental standards because economic success was based on measured output that did not take into account environmental degradation. Now that the centralized regime has collapsed, the Russian Federation is finding the implementation of environmental taxes difficult - again because the institutional structure is not well-enough developed to cope with the practical aspects of this policy.

In developing countries the importance of institutions is even more evident. Some countries have the misfortune of not having a rule of law or a respect for private property so that powerful individuals are able to appropriate the property of others. For example, under the Duvalier regimes in Haiti the so-called *Tonton Macoutes* - the president's personal police force - were given the freedom to provide for themselves by appropriating income and assets from the general population. In such a situation, the use of private property rights - or any other rights - to solve environmental problems may have little value. Indeed, institutional failure may not only prevent the solution of environmental problems but is a major factor that inhibits economic development and contributes to poverty (Grafton and Rowlands, 1996; Olson, 1996). Understanding the institutions of a country or region are, thus, fundamental to successfully applying property rights or any other approach to solving environmental challenges. For instance, the introduction of private transferable harvesting rights in small-scale, artisanal fisheries in West Africa is probably not appropriate if community rights over sedentary fish stocks already exist. Similarly, trying to introduce community rights into large-scale, commercial and developed fisheries where the resource migrates over a large area is also not recommended. The key to success is to set up an incentive structure for individuals that is compatible with both the characteristics of the resource and institutions.

But we do not have to look to the former-socialist or developing states to find problems. For one thing, developed countries have yet to implement a way to take account of their "natural" stock of capital, like resources and environmental amenities. For decades, countries have been working on how to implement a comprehensive "green accounting" system, however this has not yet fully taken place. In the absence of explicit values for our "natural capital" governments may have the incentive to overstate its size and understate any damages to it. This incentive arises from the fact that it is costly to implement environmental policies, and hence governments that are battling this decade's malaise of over-extended budgets, would be encouraged to understate, whenever possible, the magnitude of environmental problems.

Wealthy, developed countries trying to implement environmental policies also face a variety of difficulties stemming from their particular institutional structure. For instance, citizens are typically informed enough to demand, say, that hazardous wastes are properly stored; and are rich enough to demand with equal if not greater force that they **not** be stored "in their backyard". "Not In My Back Yard" ism or NIMBYISM is a formidable force with which western governments must grapple. Because of the nature of western democracy, governments cannot easily confiscate private property for such purposes without experiencing strong political backlashes. One way that governments frequently seek to minimize this type of problem is to appoint "independent" bodies that make the decisions as to where the wastes will be stored, where the garbage will be incinerated, or where the airport is to be located.

6.4   A FINAL WORD

Although it would be nice to be able to say that we've solved the world's environmental problems, we have not! Hopefully, what we have done is provide you with a coherent framework within which these problems can be analysed and better understood. If you finish this book with a sense of cautious optimism about our ability to manage our environment and learn from our mistakes then we have succeeded in our objective. While some may think that humankind is on a path towards environmental ruin, we do not. International cooperation, for instance, means that we can reasonably expect the ozone layer to reach its normal state by the year 2040. We are considerably better informed today about the environment and our impact on it than we were just a few decades ago. Becoming informed about problems is the necessary first step in the search for solutions. Although we know much more about environmental degradation and resource mismanagement in our own backyard, people are becoming much more aware of the plight of other countries, particularly those in the developing world. We now have a much clearer understanding of the role of institutional structures in framing suitable policy responses to the various challenges we face.

Solving environmental problems requires us to encourage individuals, owners of firms, or our national governments to take account of the costs that their actions impose on others. This property-rights perspective governs every facet of our book. We consider property rights - be they private, state or community-based or a mix of rights - to be of paramount importance in solving our environmental challenges. The fact that tradeable property rights have been applied successfully in a number of creative ways to target pollution and resource management problems directly, attests to their importance. The United States is using tradeable SO_2 permits to control acid rain; New Zealand, Canada, Iceland, Australia and the United States employ individual transferable quotas to better manage fisheries; and more and more countries are seriously considering tradeable property rights to encourage individuals, firms or even governments to take account of their actions on others. In addition to tradeable private rights, community and state rights have been successful at eliciting the appropriate use of the environment and resources. While we do not suggest that any one regime or mix of regimes is appropriate for all circumstances, we do believe that property rights hold the key to the protection of the common good.

Glossary

Abatement: A method or process which controls or reduces discharges and emissions of pollutants.

Acid Rain: Rain which has a pH level of 5.6 or less. A common cause of acid rain is emissions of sulphur dioxide.

Agenda 21: A document released at the 1992 Rio Summit which outlines a plan to achieve sustainable development.

Alar: A pesticide which was used by apple orchardists, among others, and was banned in the United States in 1989 following a well-publicized study that reportedly linked its use to cancer.

Alienate: The ability to transfer an asset to somebody else.

Alvarez Hypothesis: The hypothesis that the earth was hit by at least one comet some 65 million years ago which led to mass extinctions, including that of dinosaurs.

Ambient Permits: Pollution permits that specify the maximum permissible levels of pollution in the environment at defined sites.

Ambient Standard: A standard that specifies the maximum permissible concentrations of pollution in the environment.

Amenity Value: The non-commercial value that is obtained from using an aspect of the environment. Walking in a forest is an example of the amenity value of a national park.

Biodiversity: The variation that exists in all living things across species and across individuals.

Biodiversity Prospecting: The cataloguing, sampling and collection of plant and animal species.

Biochemical Oxygen Demand (BOD): The demand for oxygen in both chemical and biological processes. BOD is frequently used as a measure of the effects of wastes on water quality and is calculated by measuring the weight of oxygen removed from a given quantity of water by microorganisms over a five day period, at a constant temperature of 20 degrees Celsius.

Boreal Forest: A vast northern coniferous forest found in Canada, Alaska, Russia and Scandinavia.

Carbon Sink: The ability of plants, such as phytoplankton in the oceans and growing trees, to absorb carbon dioxide from the atmosphere.

Charge: See pollution charge.

Chlorofluorocarbons (CFCs): Chlorine and fluorine-based chemicals that were used in propellants and coolants. CFCs have been shown to contribute to the thinning of stratospheric ozone.

Closed System: A system that exchanges no matter or energy with its environment.

Club Good: A good in which users are easily able to exclude others from using, but which is congestible. An example of a club good is a library.

Coase Theorem: A theorem named after Ronald Coase, the 1991 Nobel Laureate in Economics which states that if people do not behave strategically, transactions costs are zero, and the allocation of rights does not affect the marginal valuations of individuals, then the assignment of private property rights internalize an externality. Moreover, it does not matter in terms of efficiency who receives the property right.

Command and Control: An approach for regulating pollution which often involves setting maximum permissible discharges.

Commercial Value: The value of a resource only in terms of its monetary benefits.

Common Property: A term often applied to a situation where property rights do not exist over a natural resource. It is more appropriately used to describe a set of community rights to property and resources.

Common-Pool Resources: Natural resources whose use is rivalrous but where the exclusion of users is difficult.

Commons: Common-pool resources that are managed with community rights, like community grazing rights.

Communal Rights: See community rights.

Community Rights: Property rights that exclude persons outside a well-defined community from using resources and which define rules over how resources should be exploited by members of the community.

Compliance: The act of complying with environmental and resource regulations.

Comprehensive Environmental Response, Compensation, and Liability Act (CERCLA): 42 U.S.C. ss. 9601-9657; sometimes known as the Superfund Act. Established in the United States in 1980, this act created a fund to clean up hazardous waste sites and defined the liability of firms that contributed to these sites.

Congestible: A good is congestible if, past a certain threshold, an increase in the number of users reduces the benefits enjoyed by existing users.

Conservation: The management of the environment and natural resources that considers future generations and all market and non-market values.

Consumptive Value: The value of a resource only in terms of its worth when consumed or used by people.

Contingent Valuation Method: An approach used to quantify the monetary value of environment amenities by asking individuals direct questions.

Contingent Valuation Survey: Used to elicit responses from individuals regarding their monetary value of environment amenities.

Contributory Value: The value of a resource in terms of its contribution to other resources, species and ecosystems.

Convention on Biodiversity: The 1992 convention on biological diversity which allows for the free trade of genetic resources while providing ways for rich countries to finance biodiversity conservation.

Convention on Climate Change: A convention first signed at the Rio Summit and which came into effect in 1994 with the aim of controlling the emissions of human-made greenhouse gases.

Cost-Benefit Analysis: A method by which the total benefits and costs of a project or development are calculated, taking into account the fact that future benefits and costs need to be discounted. If the net benefits (discounted benefits minus costs) are positive a project is said to have a positive net present value.

Cretaceous Period: A period on earth from around 146 to 65 million years ago.

Current Dollars: The value of returns or costs incurred at some other time (past or future) in terms of today's dollars.

Decentralized Outcome: An outcome that arises from many individuals seemingly acting independently and in their own self-interest.

Deforestation: The transformation of forest land into other uses, such as agriculture.

Desertification: A natural or human-induced process by which desert encroaches on arid or semi-arid lands.

Developing Country: A country with a low level of income, often characterized by relatively high rates of mortality and morbidity and a large proportion of its population living in rural areas.

Dichloro-diphenyl-trichloro-ethane (DDT): An organochlorine chemical used as an insecticide and which is now banned in a number of countries because of its ability to accumulate in animals high up in the food chain.

Dioxin: A toxic compound found in some herbicide and industrial wastes.

Discount Rate: The rate used to put future benefits and costs into current dollar terms.

Discounting: A method for evaluating benefits and costs in the future by valuing them in current dollars.

Divisibility: A characteristic of property rights which refers to how well its use and/or ownership can be transferred and/or split among users.

Duration: A characteristic of property rights which refers to the expected length of time the owner is able to exercise rights over the property.

Economic Development: The process by which individuals become empowered to reach their full potential. This often involves raising living standards, enlarging economic opportunities, and increasing the availability and quality of services such as health care and education.

Economic Growth: The annual increase in the total real value of goods and services produced in a country.

Ecosystem: A distinct physical environment along with the interdependent flora and fauna that live there.

Efficient Outcome: An outcome where society is doing the best it can with what it has.

Emission (Quantity) Permits: Pollution permits which specify the quantity of emissions that can be discharged by a plant and/or firm in a given period of time.

Emission Reduction Credits: Credits obtained by firms by emitting less than the maximum permissible level. In the United States these credits can be traded under certain conditions.

Endangered Species: A species that faces a very high probability of extinction in the wild in the near future.

Enforceability: The ability to enforce the various characteristics of property rights.

Entropy: An index or measure of unavailable energy in a system. It is often considered as a measure of disorder in a system.

Environmental Assessment: An interdisciplinary approach that may use many different methodologies to assess the effect of a particular project or development on the environment.

Environmental Protection Agency (EPA): The U.S. federal regulatory agency charged with enforcing the various federal laws on the environment.

Equity: The degree to which an outcome is "fair" such that consideration is given to the gains and losses of individuals.

Exclusivity: A characteristic of property rights which refers to an owner's ability to exclude others from using the given right.

Existence Value: The value of a natural resource stemming from its existence in contrast to its consumptive value.

Externality: A situation where persons do not take into account the costs imposed on others by their actions, resulting in goods and resources not being used efficiently.

Flexibility: A characteristic of property rights which refers to an owner's ability to accommodate changes in both the asset and his or her own circumstances.

Flow Pollutant: A pollutant that affects people when it is discharged but does not accumulate in the environment.

Food Chain: The transfer of food from one organism to another in a hierarchial sequence.

Fugitive Resource: A natural resource that is mobile, such as a fishery.

Global Commons: Common-pool resources which are of global importance, such as stratospheric ozone. Most global commons are treated as open access.

Global Warming: The hypothesized warming of the earth's surface temperature due to increases in the concentration of greenhouse gases in the atmosphere.

Green Accounting: An approach designed to account for the value of the environment and natural resources, and human impact upon them.

Greenhouse Effect: The idea that increased concentrations of greenhouse gases in the atmosphere will increase the earth's surface temperature.

Greenhouse Gases: Gases such as carbon dioxide, methane, water vapour, nitrous oxide, and CFCs and halons which absorb and emit infrared radiation. Increased concentrations of greenhouse gases in the atmosphere are expected to lead to global warming.

Green Revolution: The large increase in yields of certain grains, such as rice and wheat, in the 1960s and 1970s due to the widespread adoption of higher yielding varieties by farmers in developing countries.

Gross National Product (GNP): A measure of the market value of all goods and services produced in a country in one year, plus investment income received from non-residents, minus investment income paid to non-residents. Only transactions that pass through the market are included in the measure.

Habitat: The physical environment where populations of flora and fauna live.

Halons: Organic compounds containing chlorine and bromine which contribute to the depletion of stratospheric ozone.

Heavy Metals: Metals such as lead, cadmium, mercury, tin and copper which have a high atomic mass and can cause health problems at sufficiently high enough concentrations in the body.

Hydrocarbons: Compounds of hydrogen and carbon.

INBio (Instituto Nacional de Biodiversidad): A Costa Rican non-profit institute established in 1989 to ensure the conservation and wise management of Costa Rica's biodiversity.

Index of Sustainable Economic Welfare: An index that attempts to take account of environmental and resource degradation when accounting for a country's well-being.

Individual Transferable Quotas (ITQs): A private and transferable property right to a certain proportion of the total harvest or a fixed amount of fish. ITQs have been implemented in a number of countries including New Zealand, Iceland, Canada, United States and Australia.

Inflation: The percentage rise in the general price level in an economy. It is typically calculated as the percentage increase in prices over a year.

Institutions: The humanly-devised constraints that govern all social interactions.

Intergenerational Equity: The notion that the current generation should consider future generations in its actions.

Intergovernmental Panel on Climate Change (IPCC): An international group of scientists convened by the United Nations to assess the current state of knowledge about human-induced changes to the earth's climate.

Internalize: An externality is said to be internalized when individuals take into account the costs of their actions on others.

Irreversibility: The notion that certain actions can never be reversed. For example, species extinction is irreversible.

Joint and Several Strict Liability: A legal rule that makes every agent involved in a given accident liable for the full cost of damages.

Laterization: The release of metal oxides into soils due to exposure to the air. This often results in a hard brick-like soil of poor quality.

Liability: A legal rule which renders firms and individuals liable for the damages caused by their actions.

Limited-User Open Access: A property-right regime where the total harvest or yield may be fixed and the number of users is controlled but individual harvests are not.

Local Pollutant: A pollutant which has an effect only in a local area.

Loess: A particular type of soil sediment deposited by wind.

London Dumping Convention of 1972: An agreement to help prevent marine pollution and the dumping of wastes and other matter at sea.

Love Canal: A residential area in northern New York State which was declared a disaster zone after chemicals from hazardous wastes began to seep to the surface of the land.

Marginal Abatement Cost: The extra cost associated with reducing the amount of pollution by a small amount.

Marginal External Cost: The extra cost imposed on others from producing a small amount more of a good.

Marginal Private Cost: The extra cost incurred by a firm from producing a small amount more of a good.

Marginal Social Benefit: The extra benefit to society from producing a small amount more of a good.

Marginal Social Cost: The extra private and external cost associated with producing a small amount more of a good.

Methyl Mercury: A water soluble organic form of mercury which can accumulate in the bodies of organisms. At high enough levels it can cause mercury poisoning.

Minamata Disease: A debilitating disease first discovered in a bay in Japan which affects the brain and nervous system and can lead to death. It is caused by the accumulation of methyl mercury in the body.

Mobile Source of Pollution: A source of pollution that is not in a fixed location, like an automobile.

Montreal Protocol: A 1987 agreement signed by 43 countries to phase out the use of ozone-depleting substances

Natural Capital Stock: All aspects of the environment, including natural resources.

Natural Resource: Virtually anything that is not human-made and is potentially of value to humanity. Natural resources include the air we breathe, oil and gas deposits, forests and almost all aspects of the environment.

Negligence: The notion that an agent is liable for damages if he or she did not take reasonable precautions for a given set of circumstances

NIMBY: An acronym for "Not in my backyard" and refers to the desire of people not to have potentially dangerous plants and hazardous waste sites located near where they or their families live, work or play.

Nitrates: Chemical compounds containing nitrogen. An important source of water pollution is nitrate run-off from land treated with nitrogenous fertilizers.

Non-exclusive (Good or Resource): A good or resource that others cannot be prevented from using.

Nonrenewable Resource: A resource that can only be exhausted or depleted, such as oil and gas deposits.

Open Access: Sometimes called the "Tragedy of the Commons" and represents a situation where no property rights exist nor controls on the number of resource users exist.

Opportunity Cost: The cost of a good in terms of the other goods and services that must be forgone to be able to produce it.

Organic Farming: A method of farming which does not use artificial fertilizers, pesticides or herbicides.

Ozone Layer: See stratospheric ozone.

pH: A logarithmic scale which provides a measure of acidity or alkalinity. A measure less than pH7 is acidic.

Phosphates: Chemical compounds containing phosphorous which can contribute to water pollution.

Point Sources of Pollution: A source of pollution that is well-defined. A coal-fired power plant is a point source of pollution.

Polluter Pays Principle: The principle that polluters should be responsible for paying the costs to society of pollution.

Pollution: Any substance, human-made or otherwise, which has a negative affect on a defined environment at a given concentration.

Pollution Charge: A compulsory payment made by individuals or firms to a regulatory authority for emitting pollution.

Pollution Subsidy: A payment made by a regulatory authority to individuals or firms to encourage them to reduce their level of pollution.

Polychlorinated Biphenyls (PCBs): Organic compounds, often used in electrical insulation, which at high levels have been associated with health problems in mammals, including humans.

Preservation: The management of the environment and natural resources with the intent to leave them, as much as possible, in the "natural state".

Private Good: A good or resource which the owner can easily exclude others from using and which is rivalrous in use. An example of a private good is a private motor car.

Private Rights: A property-right regime where ownership of goods or resources is vested in individuals or firms.

Property Rights: The rights, entitlements and privileges of individuals or groups of individuals to use goods and resources.

Property-Rights Regime: Any one of many different combinations of characteristics of property rights and ownership structures for property rights. The main property-right regimes are limited-user open access, community rights, private rights and state rights.

Public Good: A good which is non-exclusive, non-rivalrous and not congestible. An example of a public good is a lighthouse.

Quality of Title: A characteristic of property rights which refers to the owner's *de jure* rights to the good or resource in question.

Regional Clear Air Incentives Market (RECLAIM): An emission permit trading programme in southern California that encompasses hundreds of firms and seeks to control emissions of nitrogen dioxides and sulphur dioxides into the atmosphere.

Renewable Resource: A resource which has the potential to be self-perpetuating or self-regenerating. Examples of renewable resources are forests and fisheries.

Rent: An economic term which defines the surplus received over and above all the costs of production.

Resilience: The capacity of a natural resource, population or ecosystem to absorb or adapt to change without being dramatically altered following some kind of shock, human-made or otherwise.

Resource: See natural resource.

Resource Rent: A surplus over and above the cost of production that is attributable solely to the scarcity of the resource being harvested.

Retroactive Liability: A legal rule that makes firms and individuals retroactively responsible for any damages arising from their past actions even if these actions were lawful at the time.

Rio Summit: The 1992 United Nations Conference on Environment and Development which took place in Rio de Janeiro, Brazil.

Risk: A situation where it is possible to know all possible outcomes and the probability that each outcome will arise.

Rivalrous: The notion that one person's gain is someone's loss.

Salinization: A process by which salts accumulate in soils thus reducing their fertility.

Second Law of Thermodynamics: The amount of unavailable energy (entropy) of a closed system continuously and irreversibly increases over time. Its implication is that all kinds of energy are gradually transformed into heat which eventually dissipates such that we are no longer able to use it to do work.

Soil Erosion: A natural and human-made process by which soil is dispersed via water and air.

Standard: A rule which applies uniformly across all firms or individuals.

State Rights: A property-right regime where ownership of goods and/or resources are vested in a central governing authority. State rights can co-exist with other property-right regimes.

Stationary Resource: A resource which is not mobile, such as a gold deposit.

Stock Pollutant: A pollutant which accumulates in the environment, such as DDT.

Storable Resource: A natural resource, such as water, which can be stored for later use.

Stratospheric Ozone: Three oxygen atom molecules found at heights of between 15 and 45 kilometres which help protect the earth's surface from ultraviolet radiation.

Strict Liability: A legal rule which makes firms and individuals liable for all the damages caused by their actions, irrespective of whether or not they were negligent.

Subsidy: See pollution subsidy.

Subtractable Use: The notion that one person's use of a natural resource diminishes the yield for others.

Superfund: See Comprehensive Environmental Response, Compensation, and Liability Act.

Superfund Amendments Reauthorization Act (SARA): A 1986 act which gives the legal right to people who have paid for the clean-up costs from hazardous waste sites to collect these costs from other individuals or firms who contributed to the pollution at these sites.

Sustainable: The ability of a natural resource and/or system to be self-perpetuating over time.

Sustainable Development: The notion that we should manage our planet so that future generations have the potential to be as "well off" as the current generation.

Tax: See pollution charge.

Threshold Effect: The idea that beyond a certain point or threshold a very small change to a system can have a very large effect.

Total Particulate Matter: A measure of the particles in a given volume of air.

Total Suspended Solids: A measure of the total particulate matter suspended in a liquid, usually water.

Transactions Costs: The costs of exchanging and enforcing property rights.

Transferability: A characteristic of property rights which refers to the owner(s) ability to transfer, bequest or trade ownership of the right.

Ultraviolet Radiation: Short wavelength electromagnetic radiation. Stratospheric ozone helps protects the earth's surface from ultraviolet radiation from the sun.

Uncertainty: A situation where many outcomes are possible but it is not possible to determine the probability of each outcome.

Unitization: The agreement of the joint owners of a common-pool resource to let only one individual or company exploit the resource but have the net revenues shared at an agreed-to proportion among all owners.

Vienna Convention for the Protection of the Ozone Layer: The 1985 convention which committed 36 countries to control emissions of chlorofluorocarbons.

Withdrawal Right: The right to extract a yield or harvest from a natural resource.

World Wide Web Sites

Thousands of web sites exist on many topics on the environment. The most commonly used sites are accessible from the International Environment Resources web site, http://www.contact.org/environs.htm and the Environmental Action Group site at http://www.afn.org/~eag/ links.html. We list below just a few of the more informative and interesting places to visit.

American Water Works Association (AWWA)
http://www.awwa.org/
An international non-profit scientific and educational society dedicated to the improvement of drinking water quality and supply.

Australian Environmental Resources Information Network
http://www.erin.gov.au/
Environmental information courtesy of the Australian government.

CIESIN Kiosk
http://www.ciesin.org/kiosk/subindex.html
Links to unpublished scholarly papers on environmental issues.

CNN Earth Main Page
http://www.cnn.com/EARTH/
Most-up-to date information on environmental issues by Cable News Network (CNN).

Commission on Geosciences, Environment, and Resources National Research Council:
http://www2.nas.edu/cger/
A U.S. commission that oversees and coordinates the activities of the U.S. National Research Council.

Committee for the National Institute for the Environment
http://www.cnie.org/
A U.S. non-profit organization working to improve the scientific basis for making decisions on environmental issues.

Earth Network
http://www.ecouncil.ac.cr/
A nongovernmental organization that supports and empowers people in building a sustainable future.

EcoNet
http://www.econet.apc.org/econet/
A forum for organizations and individuals working for environmental preservation and sustainability.

EELink Environmental Education on the Internet
http://www.nceet.snre.umich.edu/
Information and ideas that helps educators explore environmental issues.

Envirobiz
http://www.envirobiz.com/
An international environmental information network for businesses.

EnviroLink Library
http://www.envirolink.org/orgs/
A site that links to many environmental resources.

Environment Canada
http://www.doe.ca/envhome.html
The web site of Environment Canada.

Environmental Action Group
http://www.afn.org/~eag/links.html
Links to many environmental organizations and resources.

Environmental Defense Fund
http://www.edf.org
Web site of the Environmental Defense Fund.

Environmental Information Resources
http://www.gwu.edu/~greenu/index2.html
Numerous links to environmental resources on the internet.

Environmental Journalism Home Page
http://www.sej.org/
A forum for environmental journalists.

Environmental Monitoring and Assessment Programme
http://www.epa.gov/docs/emap/
An environmental monitoring and assessment programme administered by the U.S. Environmental Protection Agency.

Environmental News Network
http://www.enn.com/
Latest news on environmental issues.

Environmental Pollution and Control
http://www.fedworld.gov/environ.htm
Links to various organizations dealing with environmental issues.

Environmental Protection Agency
http:/www.epa.gov/
The web site of the U.S. Environmental ProtectionAgency.

Environmental Technology Gateway
http://www.nttc.edu/environmental.html
A forum that discusses the technical aspects of environmental issues.

Friends of the Earth International
http://www.xs4all.nl/~foeint/
Web site of an umbrella organization of environmental groups.

Green Disk
http://www.igc.apc.org/greendisk/
A journal of the environmental movement.

Greenpeace International
htttp://www.greenpeace.org/
An independent, campaigning organization which uses non-violent, creative
confrontation to expose global environmental problems.

Guide to the Global Environment
http://www.wri.org/wri/wr9697/index.html
World Bank web site that deals with global environmental issues.

Institute of Environmental Engineering (ICE)
http://www.englib.cornell.edu/i.../environmentalengineering.html
Links to organizations that deal with technical aspects of the environment.

International Council for Local Environmental Initiatives
http://www.iclei.org/
An international environmental agency for local governments.

International Environment Resources
http://www.contact.org/environs.htm
Links to over 150 environmental web sites around the world.

Internet and Online Resources
http://cluin.com/resourc1.htm
Links to numerous resources on environmental issues.

Lawrence Berkeley National Laboratory Energy & Environment Division
http://eande.lbl.gov/EE.html
A research centre on energy and environmental topics to advance the efficient, environmentally acceptable uses of energy.

Ministry of Environment Norway
http://www.statkart.no:80/md/
Links to various institutions, programmes relating to environmental issues.

National Defense for Environmental Excellence (NDCEE)
http://www.ndcee.ctc.com/
A U.S. organization which addresses high priority environmental problems.

National Marine Fisheries Service
http://kingfish.ssp.nmfs.gov/
Information about the programmes that support the domestic and international conservation and management of living marine resources.

New Zealand Ministry for the Environment
http://www.mfe.govt.nz/
The web site on the environment in New Zealand, courtesy of the New Zealand government.

OEPA Web Site
http://www.eh.doe.gov/oepa/top.htm
Information about a wide variety of environmental policies and strategies for protecting the public and the environment.

Pennsylvania Department of Environmental Protection
http://www.dep.state.pa.us/
A source of information on various aspects of the environment.

President's Council on Sustainable Development
http://www.whitehouse.gov/PCSD
A forum to discuss the political aspects of sustainable development.

Resources for the Future
http://www.rff.org
A premier research institute which examines problems in the environment.

Sierra Club
http://www.sierraclub.org/
A non-profit organization that promotes conservation of the natural environment.

United Kingdom Department of the Environment
http://www.open.gov.uk/doe/envir/index.htm
Information on the environment, courtesy of the U.K. government.

United Nations Development Programme
http://www.undp.org/env.html

Environment-related information on sustainable human development.

United Nations Environment Programme

http://www.unep.ch/

Information about the international treaties and major programmes dealing with the environment and sustainable development.

Usenet Environmental News Groups

http://gwis.circ.gwu.edu/~greenu/usenet.html

A list of discussion groups on the internet.

Washington State Department of Ecology

http://www.wa.gov/ecology/

The principal environmental management agency of the State of Washington.

World Bank Global Environmental Facility

http://www.worldbank.org/html/gef/gefgraph.htm

A World Bank web site with online documents on various environmental issues.

World Environment News

http://www.planet.ark.com.au/new/intro.html

A Reuters site that provides daily updates of relevant environmental news stories.

World Resources Institute

http://www.wri.org

A detailed and primary reference volume on global environmental and natural resource conditions.

World Wide Fund for Nature International (formerly World Wildlife Fund)

http://www.panda.org

Web site of the World Wide Fund for Nature.

WorldWide Web Virtual Library: Environment

http:/ecosys.drdr.virginia.edu/Environment.shtml

Links to the different areas of environment such as biodiversity, energy, ecology, sustainable development and many more!

References

Air Quality Management District (AQMD) (1996), *Advisor*, South Coast Air Quality Management District News Publication, **3** (4), March.

Allaby, M. (1996), *Basics of Environmental Science*, London: Routledge.

Andersen, L.E., C.W.L. Granger. L.-L. Huang, E.J. Reis and D. Weinhold (1996), 'Report on Amazon Deforestation', *Discussion Paper 96-40*, Department of Economics, University of California, San Diego.

Andersen, M.S. (1994), *Governance by Green Taxes, Making Pollution Prevention Pay*, Manchester: Manchester University Press.

Anderson, T.L. and D.R. Leal (1991), *Free Market Environmentalism*, San Francisco: Pacific Institute for Public Policy.

Annala, J.H. (1996), 'New Zealand's ITQ System; Have the First Eight Years Been a Success or a Failure?' *Reviews in Fish Biology and Fisheries,* **6**, 43-62.

Arnold, F.S. (1994), *Economic Analysis of Environmental Policy and Regulation*, New York: John Wiley and Sons.

Baarschers, W.H. (1996), *Eco-Facts and Eco-Fiction: Understanding the Environmental Debate*, New York: Routledge.

Bailey, R. (ed) 1995, *The True State of the Planet*, New York: The Free Press.

Balling, R.C., Jr. (1995), 'Global Warming: Messy Models, Decent Data and Pointless Policy', in R. Bailey (ed), *The True State of the Planet*, New York: The Free Press, pp. 83-108.

Barbier, E.B., J.C. Burgess and C. Folke (1994), *Paradise Lost? The Ecological Economics of Biodiversity*, London: Earthscan Publications Ltd.

Barbier, E.B. and M. Rauscher (1994), 'Trade, Tropical Deforestation and Policy Interventions', *Environmental and Resource Economics*, **4**, 75-94.

Barzel, Y. (1989), *Economic Analysis of Property Rights*, New York: Cambridge University Press.

Baumol, W.J. and W.E. Oates (1988), *The Theory of Environmental Policy* (second edition), Cambridge: Cambridge University Press.

Baumol, W.J and W.E. Oates (1995), 'Long-Run Trends in Environmental Quality', in J.L. Simon (ed), *The State of Humanity*, Cambridge, Mass.: Basil Blackwell, pp. 444-475.

Beinart, W. and P. Coates (1995), *Environment and History: The Taming of Nature in the USA and South Africa*, London: Routledge.

Bender, D.L. and B. Leone (1991), *The Environmental Crisis: Opposing Viewpoints*, San Diego, CA: Greenhaven Press.

Benedick, R.E. (1991), 'Protecting the Ozone Layer: New Directions in Diplomacy', in J. Mathews *et al.* (eds), *Preserving the Global Environment: The Challenge of Shared Leadership*, New York: W.W. Norton, pp. 113-153.

Berrill, M. (1997), *The Plundered Seas*, Vancouver, BC: Greystone Books.

Berkes, F. (1986), 'Local-level Management and the Commons Problem: A Comparative Study of Turkish Coastal Fisheries', *Marine Policy,* **10**, 215-229.

Berkes, F. (ed) (1989), *Common Property Resources: Ecology and Community-Based Sustainable Development*, London: Bellhaven Press.

Bernards, Neal (ed) (1991), *The Environmental Crisis: Opposing Viewpoints*, San Diego: Greenhaven Press.

Bernstam, Mikhail S. (1995), 'Comparative Trends in Resource Use and Pollution in Market and Socialist Economies', in J.L. Simon (ed), *The State of Humanity*, Cambridge, MA: Basil Blackwell, pp. 503-522.

Bertram, G. (1992), 'Tradeable Emission Permits and the Control of Greenhouse Gases', *Journal of Development Studies,* **28**, 423-446.

Bishop, R.C., P.A. Champ and D.J. Mullarkey (1995), 'Contingent Valuation', in D.W. Bromley (ed), *The Handbook of Environmental Economics*, Oxford: Basil Blackwell, pp. 629-654.

Brannlund, R., R. Fare and S. Grosskopf (1995), *Environmental and Resource Economics*, **6** (1), 23-36.

Bridges, O. and J.W. Bridges (1996), *Losing Hope: The Environment and Health in Russia*, Aldershot: Ashgate Publishing.

Bromley, D.W. (1989), 'Property Relations and Economic Development: The Other Land Reform', *World Development*, **17**, 867-877.

Bromley, D.W. (1991), *Environment and Economy: Property Rights and Public Policy*, Oxford: Basil Blackwell.

Bromley, D.W. (ed) (1992), *Making the Commons Work: Theory, Practice, and Policy*, San Francisco: Institute for Contemporary Studies.

Bromley, D.W. (ed) (1995), *The Handbook of Environmental Economics*, Oxford: Blackwell.

Bromley, D.W. and D.P. Chapagain (1984), 'The Village against the Center: Resource Depletion in South Asia', *American Journal of Agricultural Economics*, **66**, 868-873.

Browder, J.O. (1988), 'Public Policy and Deforestation in the Brazilian Amazon', in R. Repetto and M. Gillis (eds), *Public Policies and the Misuse of Forest Resources*, New York: Cambridge University Press, pp. 247-298.

Brown, G.M., Jr., and R.W. Johnson (1984), 'Pollution Control by Effluent Charges: It Works in the Federal Republic of Germany, Why Not in the U.S?', *Natural Resources Journal*, **24**, October 1984, 929-966.

Brown, K. and D. Pearce (eds) (1994), *The Causes of Tropical Deforestation: The Economic and Statistical Analysis of Factors Giving Rise to the Loss of Tropical Forests*, Vancouver, BC: University of British Columbia Press.

Brown, L.R. (1995), 'Nature's Limits', in L.R. Brown (ed), *State of the World 1995*, New York: W.W. Norton and Company, pp. 3-20.

Brown, L.R. (ed) (1996), *State of the World 1996*, New York: W.W. Norton and Company.

Brown, S., D. Donovan, B. Fisher, K. Hanslow, M. Hinchy, M. Mathewson, C. Polidano, V. Tulpulé, and S. Wear (1997), *The Economic Impact of International Climate Change Policy,* Canberra: Australian Bureau of Agricultural and Resource Economics.

Brubaker, E. (1995) *Property Rights in the Defence of Nature*, Toronto: Earthscan Canada.

Bruce, J.P., H. Lee and E.F. Haites (1996), *Climate Change 1995: Economic and Social Dimensions of Climate Change*, published for the Intergovernmental Panel on Climate Change, Cambridge: Cambridge University Press.

Budiansky, S. (1995), *Nature's Keepers: The New Science of Naure Management*, New York: The Free Press.

Callan, S. and J.M. Thomas (1996), *Environmental Economics and Management*, Boston: Richard D. Irwin.

Carson, R.T., R.C. Mitchell, W.M. Hanemann, R.J. Kopp, S. Presser, and P.A. Ruud (1994), 'Contingent Valuation and Lost Passive Use: Damages from the Exxon Valdez', *Discussion Paper 94-18*, Washington, DC: Resources for the Future.

Carter, L.J. (1987), *Nuclear Imperatives and Public Trust*, Washington, DC: Resources for the Future.

Chiras, D.D. (1994), *Environmental Science: Action for a Sustainable Future* (fourth edition), Redwood City, CA: Benjamin/Cummings Publishing Company.

Ciriacy-Wantrup, S.V. (1968), *Resource Conservation: Economics and Policies*, (third edition), Berkeley, CA: University of California Agricultural Experimental Station.

Ciriacy-Wantrup, S.V. and R.C. Bishop (1975), 'Common Property as a Concept in Natural Resources Policy', *Natural Resources Journal,* **15**, 713-727.

Cline, W.R. (1992a), *The Economics of Global Warming*, Washington, DC: Institute for International Economics.

Cline, W.R. (1992b), *Global Warming: Estimating the Benefits of Abatement*, Paris: Organisation for Economic Co-operation and Development.

Coase, R.N. (1960), 'The Problem of Social Cost', *Journal of Law and Economics*, **3**, 1-44.

Cooter, R. and T. Ulen (1988), *Law and Economics*, Illinois: Scott, Foresman and Company.

Costanza, R. and C. Folke (1996), 'The Structure and Function of Ecological Systems in Relation to Property-Rights Regimes', in S.S. Hanna, C. Folke and K.-G. Maler (eds), *Rights to Nature: Ecological, Economic, Cultural, and Political Principles of Institutions for the Environment*, Washington, DC: Island Press, pp. 13-34.

Coull, J.R. (1993), *World Fisheries Resources*, London: Routledge.

Crabbé, P. (undated), 'Sustainable Development: Concepts, Measures, Market and Policy Failures at the Open Economy, Industry and Firm Levels', *Research Paper*, Institute for Research on Environment and Economy, University of Ottawa, Ontario, Canada.

Cropper, M.L. and W.E. Oates (1992), 'Environmental Economics: A Survey', *Journal of Economic Literature,* **30**, 700-721.

Dales, J.H. (1968), *Pollution, Property and Prices: An Essay in Policy-Making and Economics*, Toronto: University of Toronto Press.

Daly, H.E. and J.B. Cobb, Jr. (1994), *For the Common Good*, Boston: Beacon Press.

Dasgupta, P. (1982), *The Control of Resources*, Cambridge, MA: Harvard University Press.

Dasgupta, P. (1995), 'The Population Problem: Theory and Evidence', *Journal of Economic Literature,* **33**, 1879-1902.

Davis, C. (1988), 'Approaches to the Regulation of Hazardous Wastes', *Environmental Law*, **18** (3), 505-535.

Devlin, R.A. and R.Q. Grafton (1994), 'Tradeable Permits, Missing Markets, and Technology', *Environmental and Resource Economics*, **4**, 171-186.

Dewees, D.N. (1992a), 'Tort Law and the Deterrence of Environmental Pollution', in T. Tietenberg (ed), *Innovation in Environmental Policy*, New Horizons in Economics Series, Aldershot: Edward Elgar, pp. 139-164.

Dewees, D.N. (1992b), 'The Role of Tort Law in Controlling Environmental Pollution', *Canadian Public Policy*, **18** (4), 425-442.

Diamond, J. (1995), 'Easter's End', *Discover*, August, 63-6 and http://www.enews.com/magazines/discover/magtxt/080195-5.html

Dorfman, R. and N.S. Dorfman (eds) (1993), *Economics of the Environment: Selected Readings* (third edition), New York: W.W. Norton and Company.

Dornbusch, R. and J. Poterba (eds) (1991), *Global Warming: Economic Policy Responses*, Cambridge, MA: The MIT Press.

Duraiappah, A. (1996), 'Poverty and Environmental Degradation: A Literature Review and Analysis', CREED Working Paper Series No. 8, International Institute for Environment and Development, London.

Dwyer, J.P. (1993), 'The Use of Market Incentives in Controlling Air Pollution: California's Marketable Permits Program', *Ecology Law Quarterly*, **20** (103), 103-117.

Dwyer, J.P. and I. Hodge (1992), 'The Collective Management of Land for Environmental Benefit: An Examination of UK Trusts', Land Economy Discussion Paper 37, Department of Land Economy, University of Cambridge.

Dwyer, J.P. and I. Hodge (1996), *Countryside in Trust: Land Management by Conservation, Recreation and Amenity Organisations*, Chichester: John Wiley and Sons Ltd.

Easterbrook, G. (1995), *A Moment on Earth: The Coming Age of Environmental Optimism*, New York: Penguin Books.

Edwards, S.R. (1995), 'Conserving Biodiversity: Resources of Our Future', in R. Bailey (ed), *The True State of the Planet*, New York: The Free Press, pp. 211-266.

Eggertsson, T. (1996), 'The Economics of Control and the Cost of Property Rights', in S.S. Hanna, C. Folke and K.-G. Maler (eds), *Rights to Nature: Ecological, Economic, Cultural, and Political Principles of Institutions for the Environment*, Washington, DC: Island Press, pp. 157-175.

Elliott, J.A. (1994), *An Introduction to Sustainable Development*, London: Routledge.

Ellsaesser, H.W. (1995), 'Trends in Air Pollution in the United States', in J.L. Simon (ed), *The State of Humanity*, Cambridge, MA: Basil Blackwell, pp.

491-502.

Eskeland, G. (1992), 'Attacking Air Pollution in Mexico City', *Finance and Development*, **29** (4), 28-30.

Fass, R.C. (1988), 'Nuclear Waste Disposal Policy: Socioeconomic Impact of Management Issues', in G.M. Johnston *et al.* (eds), Boulder: Westview Press, pp. 91-111.

Fearnside, P.M. (1990), 'The Rate and Extent of Deforestation in Brazilian Amazonia', *Environmental Conservation,* **22**, 213-236.

Feshbach, M. (1995), 'Mortality and Health in the former Soviet Union', in J.L. Simon (ed), *The State of Humanity*, Cambridge, MA: Basil Blackwell, pp. 85-90.

Feshbach, M. and A. Friendly, Jnr. (1992), *ECOCIDE in the USSR*, New York: HarperCollins.

Field, B.C. and N.D. Olewiler (1995), *Environmental Economics*, Toronto: McGraw-Hill-Ryerson Ltd.

Flavin, C. (1996), 'Facing up to the Risks of Climate Change', in L.R. Brown (ed), *The State of the World 1996*, New York: W.W Norton and Company.

Foose, T.J. (1993), 'Riders of the Lost Ark: The Role of Captive Breeding in Conservation Strategies', in L. Kaufman and K. Mallory (eds), *The Last Extinction* (second edition), Cambridge, MA: The MIT Press, pp. 149-178.

Forrest, A.S. (1995), 'Turning Points: The Development-Environment Relationship', Research Brief No. 5, Environmental Law Institute, Washington, DC.

Forsund, F.R. and E. Naevdal (1994), 'Trading Sulfur Emissions in Europe', in G. Klaassen and F.R. Forsund (eds), *Economic Instruments for Pollution Control*, The Netherlands: Kluwer Academic Publishers, pp. 231-248.

Forsund, F.R. and S. Strom (1988), *Environmental Economics and Management: Pollution and Natural Resources*, London: Croom Helm.

Fullerton, D. and T. Kinnaman (1996), 'Household Responses to Pricing Garbage by the Bag', *American Economic Review*, **86** (4), 971-984.

Gangadharan, L. (1997), 'Transaction Costs in Tradeable Emissions Markets: An Empirical Study of the Regional Clean Air Incentives Market in Los Angeles', unpublished mimeo, University of Southern California, Department of Economics, 42 pages.

Garber. E.J. (1987), 'Federal Common Law of Contribution under the 1986 CERCLA Amendments', **14** (1), 365-388.

Georgescu-Roegen, N. (1975), 'Energy and Economic Myths', *Southern Economic Journal,* **41**, 347-381.

Glass, E.A. (1988), 'Superfund and SARA: Are there any Defenses Left?',

Harvard Environmental Law Review, **12** (2), 385-463.

Goeller, H.E. (1995), 'Trends in Nonrenewable Resources', in J.L. Simon (ed), *The State of Humanity*, Cambridge, MA: Basil Blackwell, pp. 313-322.

Gollin, M.A. (1993), 'The Convention on Bilogical Diversity and Intellectual Property Rights', in W.V. Reid, S.A. Laird, C.A. Meyer, R. Gomez, A. Sittenfield, D.H. Janzen, M.A. Gollin and C. Juma (eds), *Biodiversity Prospecting: Using Genetic Resources for Sustainable Development*, Baltimore, MD: World Resources Institute, pp. 289-302.

Golub, A. and E. Strukova (1994), 'Application of a Pollution Fee System in Russia', in G. Klaassen and F.R. Forsund (eds), *Economic Instruments for Pollution Control*, The Netherlands: Kluwer Academic Publishers, pp. 165-184.

Goodland, R. (1992), 'The Case that the World has Reached Limits', in R. Goodland, H.E. Daly and S. El Serafy (eds), *Population, Technology, and Lifestyle*, Washington, DC: Island Press, pp. 3-22.

Goodland, R., H.E. Daly and S. El Serafy (eds) (1992), *Population, Technology, and Lifestyle*, Washington, DC: Island Press.

Goodland, R. and V. Edmundson (eds) (1994), *Environmental Assessment and Development*, Washington, DC: World Bank.

Goudie,A. (1994), *The Human Impact on the Natural Environment*, Cambridge, Mass.: The MIT Press.

Grafton, R.Q. (1995), 'Rent Capture in a Rights-Based Fishery', *Journal of Environmental Economics and Management*, **28**, 48-67.

Grafton, R.Q. (1996a), 'Individual Transferable Quotas: Theory and Practice', *Reviews in Fish Biology and Fisheries*, **6**, 5-20.

Grafton (1996b), 'Implications of Taxing Quota Value in an Individual Transferable Quota Fishery: A Comment', *Marine Resource Economics*, **11**, 125-127.

Grafton, R.Q. (1996c), 'Performance of and Prospects for Rights-Based Fisheries Management in Atlantic Canada', in B. Crowley (ed), *Taking Ownership: Property Rights and Fishery Management on the Atlantic Coast*, Halifax: Atlantic Institute for Market Studies, pp. 145-181.

Grafton, R.Q. (1997), 'Private, Community, and State Rights: Achieving the Right Mix', Department of Economics Working Paper 9701E, University of Ottawa.

Grafton, R.Q. and R.A. Devlin (1996), 'Paying for Pollution: Permits and Charges', *Scandinavian Journal of Economics*, **98**, 275-288.

Grafton, R.Q. and D. Rowlands (1996), 'Development Impeding Institutions: The Political Economy of Haiti', *Canadian Journal of Development Studies*,

17, 261-277.

Grafton, R.Q. and J. Silva-Echenique (1997), 'How to Manage Nature? Strategies, Predator-Prey Models and Chaos', *Marine Resource Economics,* **12**, 127-143.

Grafton, R.Q., D. Squires and K.J. Fox (1997), 'Private Property and Economic Efficiency: A Study of a Common-Pool Resource', paper presented at the Symposium on the Efficiency of North Atlantic Fisheries in Reykjavik, Iceland September 12 and 13, 1997.

Grafton, R.Q., D. Squires and J.E. Kirkley (1996), 'Private Property Rights and Crises in World Fisheries: Turning the Tide?', *Contemporary Economic Policy* **14**, 90-99.

Hahn, R.W. (1988), 'An Evaluation of Options for Reducing Hazardous Waste', *The Harvard Environmental Law Review,* **12** (1), 201-230.

Hahn, R.W. and G.L. Hester (1989), 'Where did all the Markets Go? An Analysis of EPA's Emissions Trading Programme', *Yale Journal of Regulation,* **6**, 109-120.

Hanley, N. (1989), 'Valuing Non-Market Goods using Contingent Valuation', *Journal of Economic Surveys,* **3**, 235-252.

Hanley, N. and C.L. Spash (1993), *Cost-Benefit Analysis and the Environment,* Cheltenham: Edward Elgar.

Hanna, S., C. Folke and K.-G. Maler (eds) (1996), *Rights to Nature: Cultural, Economic, Political and Ecological Principles of Institutions for the Environment,* Washington, DC: Island Press.

Hanna, S. and M. Munasinghe (eds) (1995), *Property Rights in a Social and Ecological Context: Case Studies and Design Applications,* Washington, DC: The World Bank.

Hardin, G. (1968), 'The Tragedy of the Commons', *Science,* **162**, 1143-1248.

Heal, Geoffrey (1992), 'International Negotiations on Emission Control', *Structural Change and Economic Dynamics,* **3** (2), 223-240.

Hodge, I. (1995a), *Environmental Economics,* London: Macmillan.

Hodge, I. (1995b), 'Public Policies for Land Conservation', in D.W. Bromley (ed), *The Handbook of Environmental Economics,* Cambridge, MA: Basil Blackwell, pp. 89-107.

Holling, C.S. (1973), 'Resilience and Stability of Ecological Systems', *Annual Review of Ecology and Systematics,* **4**, 1-23.

Holling, C.S. and S. Sanderson (1996), 'Dynamics of (Dis)harmony in Ecological and Social Systems', in S.S. Hanna, C. Folke and K.-G. Maler (eds), *Rights to Nature: Ecological, Economic, Cultural, and Political Principles of Institutions for the Environment,* Washington, DC: Island Press, pp. 57-85.

Holling, C.S., D.W. Schindler, B.W. Walker and J. Roughgarden (1995), 'Biodiversity in the Functioning of Ecosystems: An Ecological Synthesis', in C. Perrings, K.-G. Maler, C. Folke, C.S. Holling and B-O Jansson (eds), *Biodiversity Loss: Economic and Ecological Issues*, Cambridge: Cambridge University Press, pp. 44-83.

Howe, C.W. (1994), 'Taxes *versus* Tradeable Discharge Permits: A Review in the Light of the U.S. and European Experience', *Environmental and Resource Economics*, **4** (2), 151-170.

Hutchings, J.A. and R.A. Myers (1994), 'What can be Learned from the Collapse of a Renewable Resource? Atlantic Cod, Gadhus Morhua, of Newfoundland and Labrador', *Canadian Journal of Fisheries and Aquatic Sciences,* **51**, 2126-2146.

Imhoff, K.R. (1995), 'Water Pollution Control Measures and Water Quality Development in the Ruhr Catchment 1972-1992', *Water Science Technology*, **32** (5-6), 209-216.

Information on Climate Change (IUCC), United Nations Environment Programme, *Fact Sheets*, various issues, Châtelaine, Switzerland.

Jablonski, D. (1993), 'Mass Extinctions: New Answers, New Questions', in L. Kaufman and K. Mallory (eds), *The Last Extinction* (second edition), Cambridge, MA: The MIT Press, pp. 47-68.

Jacobs, M. (1991), *The Green Economy: Environment, Sustainable Development and the Politics of the Future*, London and Concord, MA: Pluto Press.

James, D. (1994), *The Application of Economic Techniques in Environmental Impact Assessment*, London: Kluwer Academic Publishers.

Johansson, P.-O. (1990), 'Valuing Environmental Damage', *Oxford Review of Economic Policy,* **6**, 34-50.

Josephy, A.M., Jr. (1994), *500 Nations: An Illustrated History of North American Indians*, New York: Alfred A. Knopf.

Kaufman, L. and K. Mallory (eds) (1993), *The Last Extinction* (second edition), Cambridge, MA: The MIT Press.

Kaufman, W. (1994), *No Turning Back: Dismantling the Fantasies of the Environmental Movement*, New York: Basic Books.

Kitabatake, Y. (1992), 'What Can Be Learned from Domestic and International Aspects of Japan's Forest Resource Utilization?', *Natural Resources Journal*, **32**, 855-881.

Klaassen, G. and F.R. Forsund (eds) (1994), *Economic Instruments for Air Pollution Control*, Dordrecht: Kluwer Academic Publishers.

Krishnan, R., J.M. Harris and N.R. Goodwin (eds) (1995), *A Survey of Ecological Economics*, Washington DC: Island Press.

Krutilla, J.V. (1967), 'Conservation Reconsidered', *American Economic Review,* **57**, 777-786.

Kudo, A. and S. Miyahara (1992), 'Predicted Restoration of the Surrounding Marine Environment after an Artificial Mercury Decontamination at Minamata Bay, Japan - Economic Values for Natural and Artificial Processes', *Water Science Technology,* **25**, 141-148.

Kulp, J.L. (1995), 'Acid Rain', in J.L. Simon (ed), *The State of Humanity*, Cambridge, MA: Basil Blackwell, pp. 523-536.

Laplante, B. and J. Lambert (1994), 'Tarification à l'Unité des Déchets Municipaux: Expériences et Discussion', *Canadian Public Policy/Analyse de Politique,* **20** (2), 165-176.

Laplante, B. and P. Rilstone (1996), 'Environmental Inspections and Emissions of the Pulp and Paper Industry in Quebec', *Journal of Environmental Economics and Management,* **31** (1), 19-36.

Libecap, G.D. (1989), *Contracting for Property Rights*, New York: Cambridge University Press.

Libecap, G.D. and S.N. Wiggins (1985), 'The Influence of Private Contractual Failure on Regulation: The Case of Oil Field Unitization', *Journal of Political Economy,* **93**, 690-714.

Luken, R.A. (1990), *Efficiency in Environmental Regulation*, Boston: Kluwer Academic Publishers.

Mabey, N., S. Hall, C. Smith and S. Gupta (eds) (1997), *Argument in the Greenhouse,* London: Routledge.

MacGillivray, P. (1986), 'Evaluation of Area Licensing in the British Columbia Roe Herring Fishery: 1981-1985', in N. Mollett (ed), *Fishery Access Control Programs Worldwide*, Fairbanks: University of Alaska, pp. 251-274.

Martin, P. (1967), 'Prehistoric Overkill', in P.S. Martin and H.E. Wright (eds), *Pleistocene Extinctions*, New Haven, Conn.: Yale University Press.

Matsuo, N. (1997), 'Key Elements Related to the Emissions Trading for the Kyoto Protocol', unpublished mimeo, The Institute of Energy Economics, Japan, 16 pages.

May, R.M. (1988), 'How Many Species are There on Earth?', *Science,* **241**, 1441-1449.

McCay, B.J. (1996), 'Common and Private Concerns', in S.S. Hanna, C. Folke and K.-G. Maler (eds), *Rights to Nature: Ecological, Economic, Cultural, and Political Principles of Institutions for the Environment*, Washington, DC: Island Press, pp. 111-126.

McClain, K.T. (1995), 'Recycling Programs', in D.W. Bromley (ed), *The Handbook of Environmental Economics*, Oxford: Blackwell, pp. 222-239.

Meadows, D.H., D.L. Meadows, J. Randers and W.W. Behrens III (1972), *The Limits to Growth* (second edition), New York: Signet.

Mendelsohn, R. (1994), 'Property Rights and Tropical Deforestation', *Oxford Economic Papers*, **46**, 750-756.

Meshkati, N. (1991), 'Human Factors in Large Scale Technological Systems' Accidents: Three Mile Island, Bhopal, Chernobyl', *Industrial Crisis Quarterly*, **5**, 131-154.

Metrick, A. and M.L. Weitzman (1996), 'Patterns of Behavior in Endangered Species Preservation', *Land Economics,* **72**, 1-16.

Michaels, P.J. (1995), 'The Greenhouse Effect and Global Change: Review and Reappraisal', in J.L. Simon (ed), *The State of Humanity*, Cambridge, MA: Basil Blackwell, pp. 544-564.

Moore, C. (1980), 'Implementation of Transferable Discharge Permits when Permit Levels Vary According to Flow and Temperature', *mimeo*, Paper Supervised by W. David and E. Joeres, University of Wisconsin-Madison, Madison WI.

Moore, S. (1995), 'The Coming Age of Abundance', in R. Bailey (ed), *The True State of the Planet*, New York: The Free Press, pp. 109-139.

Moorehead, R. (1989), 'Changes taking Place in Common-Property Resource Management in the Inland Niger Delta of Mali', in F. Berkes (ed), *Common Property Resources: Ecology and Community-Based Sustainable Development*, London: Bellhaven Press, pp. 256-272.

Morrison, D.C. (1992), 'Heavy Metal', *National Journal*, **11**, 662.

Myers, J.G., S. Morore and J.L. Simon (1995), 'Trends in Availability of Non-Fuel Minerals', in J.L. Simon (ed), *The State of Humanity*, Cambridge, MA: Basil Blackwell, pp. 303-312.

Myers, N. (1993), 'Sharing the Earth with the Whales', in L. Kaufman and K. Mallory (eds), *The Last Extinction* (second edition), Cambridge, MA: The MIT Press, pp. 179-194.

Nadis, S. (1996), 'The Environment: The Sub-Seabed Solution', *Atlantic Monthly,* October 1996, pp. 28-39.

Neal, P. (1989), *The Greenhouse Effect and Ozone Layer*, London: Dryad Press.

Neher, P.A., R. Arnason and N. Mollett (1989), *Rights Based Fishing*, Dordrecht: Kluwer Academic Publishers.

Nelson, R.H. (1995), 'Trends in Availability and Usage of Outdoor Recreation', in J.L. Simon (ed), *The State of Humanity*, Cambridge, MA: Basil Blackwell, pp. 323-327.

Nisbet, E.G. (1991), *Leaving Eden To Protect and Manage the Earth*, New York: Cambridge University Press.

Nordhaus, W.D. (1991), 'The Cost of Slowing Climate Change: A Survey', *The Energy Journal,* **12**, 37-65.

Nordhaus, W.D. (1993), *Managing the Global Commons: The Economics of Climate Change*, Cambridge, MA: The MIT Press.

Northwest Colorado Council of Governments (1984), *Point Sources - Nonpoint Sources Trading in the Lake Dillon Watershed*, Final Report, Frisco, Colorado, September 1984.

Oates, W.E. (ed) (1992), *The Economics of the Environment*, Aldershot: Edward Elgar.

Oldeman, L.R., R.T.A. Hakkeling and W.G. Sombroek (1990), *World Map of the Status of Human-Induced Soil Degradation: An Explanatory Note* (second edition), Wageningen, The Netherlands: International Soil Reference and Information Center.

Olson, M., Jr. (1996), 'Big Bills Left on the Sidewalk: Why Some Nations are Rich, and Others Poor', *Journal of Economic Perspectives,* **10**, 3-24.

O'Neil, W.B. (1983), 'Transferable Discharge Permit Trading Under Varying Stream Conditions: A Simulation of Multiperiod Permit Market Performance on the Fox River, Wisconsin', *Water Resources Research,* **19** (3), 608-612.

Organisation for Economic Co-operation and Development (OECD) (1980), *Pollution Charges in Practice*, Paris: OECD.

Organisation for Economic Co-operation and Development (OECD) (1991), *Environmental Policy: How to Apply Economic Instruments*, Paris: OECD.

Organisation for Economic Co-operation and Development (OECD) (1992a), *Economic Instruments for Environmental Management in Developing Countries*, Paris: OECD.

Organisation for Economic Co-operation and Development (OECD) (1992b), *Convention on Climate Change: Economic Aspects of Negotiations*, Paris: OECD.

Organisation for Economic Co-operation and Development (OECD) (1992c), *Market and Government Failures in Environmental Management: The Case of Transport*, Paris: OECD.

Organisation for Economic Co-operation and Development (OECD) (1993), *International Economic Instruments and Climate Change*, Paris: OECD.

Ostrom, E., R. Gardner and J. Walker (1994), *Rules, Games and Common-Pool Resources*, Ann Arbor: The University of Michigan Press.

Ostrom, E. (1988), 'Institutional Arrangements and the Commons Dilemma', in V. Ostrom, D. Feeny and H. Picht (eds), *Rethinking Institutional Analysis and Development*, San Francisco: International Center for Economic Growth, pp. 101-139.

Ostrom, E. (1990), *Governing the Commons: The Evolution of Institutions for Collective Action*, Cambridge: Cambridge University Press.

Ostrom, E. and E. Schlager (1996), 'The Formation of Property Rights', in S.S. Hanna, C. Folke and K.-G. Maler (eds), *Rights to Nature: Ecological, Economic, Cultural, and Political Principles of Institutions for the Environment*, Washington, DC: Island Press, pp. 127-156.

Page, T. (1977), *Conservation and Economic Efficiency: An Approach to Materials Policy*, Baltimore: The Johns Hopkins University Press.

Panayotou, T. (1993), *Green Markets: The Economics of Sustainable Development*, San Francisco: Institute for Contempory Studies Press.

Park, C.C. (1992), *Tropical Rainforests*, New York: Routledge.

Parson, E.A. (1993), 'Protecting the Ozone Layer', in P.M. Haas, R.O. Keohane and M.A. Levy (eds), *Institutions for The Earth: Sources of Effective International Environmental Protection*, Cambridge, MA: The MIT Press, pp 27-74.

Paterson, M. (1996), *Global Warming and Global Politics*, London: Routledge.

Pearce, D. and G. Atkinson (1995), 'Measuring Sustainable Development', in D.W. Bromley (ed), *The Handbook of Environmental Economics*, Oxford: Basil Blackwell, pp. 166-181.

Pearce, D., E. Barbier and A. Markandya (1990), *Sustainable Development: Economics and Environment in the Third World*, Aldershot: Edward Elgar.

Pearce, D.W. and R.K. Turner (1990), *Economics of Natural Resources and the Environment*, Baltimore: The Johns Hopkins University Press.

Perrings, Charles (1989), 'Environmental Bonds and Environmental Research in Innovative Activities', *Ecological Economics*, **1**, 95-110.

Perrings, C., K.-G. Maler, C. Folke, C.S. Holling and B.-O. Jansson (1995), *Biodiversity Loss: Economic and Ecological Issues*, Cambridge: Cambridge University Press.

Pickering, K.T. and L.A. Owen (1994), *An Introduction to Global Environmental Issues*, London: Routledge.

Pinkerton, E.W. (1994), 'Local Fisheries Co-management: A Review of International Experiences and their Implications for Salmon Management in British Columbia', *Canadian Journal of Fisheries and Aquatic Sciences,* **51**, 2363-2378.

Ponting, C. (1991), *A Green History of the World*, London: Sinclair-Stevenson Limited.

Portney, P.R. (1993), 'EPA and the Evolution of Federal Regulations', in R. Dorfman and N.S. Dorfman (eds), *Economics of the Environment: Selected Readings*, (Third edition)New York: W.W. Norton and Compnay, pp. 57-73.

Pradhan, A.S. and P.J. Parks (1995), 'Environmental and Socioeconomic Linkages of Deforestation and Forest land Use Change in the Nepal Himalaya', in S. Hanna and M. Munasinghe (eds.), *Property Rights in a Social and Ecological Context: Case Studies and Design Applications*, Washington, DC: International Bank for Reconstruction and Development, pp. 167-180.

Prance, G.T. (1993), 'The Amazon: Paradise Lost?', , in L. Kaufman and K. Mallory (eds), *The Last Extinction*, (second edition), Cambridge, Mass.: The MIT Press, pp. 69-114.

Pratt, L. and I. Urquhart (1994), *The Last Great Forest: Japanese Multinationals and Alberta's Northern Forests*, Edmonton, Alberta: NeWest Publishers.

Randall, A. (1987), *Resource Economics: An Economic Approach to Natural Resource and Environmental Policy*, New York: John Wiley and Son.

Redefining Progress (1995), *The General Progress Indicator: Summaries of Data and Methodologies*, San Francisco: Redefining Progress.

Rees, J. (1985), *Natural Resources: Allocation, Economics and Policy*, London: Methuen.

Regier, H.A., R.V. Mason and F. Berkes (1989), 'Reforming the Use of Natural Resources', in F. Berkes, F. (ed), *Common Property Resources: Ecology and Community-Based Sustainable Development*, London: Bellhaven Press, pp. 110-126.

Reid, W.V., S.A. Laird, C.A. Meyer, R. Gomez, A. Sittenfield, D.H. Janzen, M.A. Gollin and C. Juma (1993), *Biodiversity Prospecting: Using Genetic Resources for Sustainable Development*, Baltimore, MD: World Resources Institute.

Repetto, R. and M. Gillis (eds) (1988), *Public Policies and the Misuse of Forest Resources*, Cambridge: Cambridge University Press.

Rettig, R.B. (1995), 'Management Regimes in Ocean Fisheries', in D.W. Bromley (ed), *The Handbook of Environmental Economics*, Oxford: Basil Blackwell.

Rico, R. (1995), 'The U.S. Allowance Trading System for Sulphur Dioxide: An Update on Market Experience', *Environmental and Resource Economics*, 5(2), 115-129.

Sadler, B. (1994), 'Environmental Assessment and Development Policymaking', in R. Goodland and V. Edmundson (eds), *Environmental Assessment and Development*, Washington D.C: World Bank, pp. 3-19.

Sandler, T. (1993), 'Tropical Deforestation: Markets and Market Failures', *Land Economics*, **69**, 225-233.

Schelling, T.C. (1993), 'Some Economics of Global Warming', in R. Dorman and N.S. Dorfman (eds), *Economics of the Environment: Selected Readings*, New York, W.W. Norton and Company, pp. 464-483.

Schmid, A.A. (1995), 'The Environment and Property Rights Issues', in D.W. Bromley (ed), *The Handbook of Environmental Economics*, Oxford: Blackwell, pp. 45-60.

Scott, A.D. (1955), *Natural Resources: The Economics of Conservation*, Toronto: University of Toronto Press.

Scott, A.D. (1989), 'Evolution of Individual Transferable Quotas as a Distinct Class of Property Right', in H. Campbell, K. Menze and G. Waugh (eds), *Economics of Fisheries Management in the Pacific Islands Region*, Canberra: Australian Centre for International Agricultural Research, pp. 51-67.

Scott, A.D. and J. Johnson (1985), 'Property Rights: Developing the Characteristics of Interests in Natural Resources', in A.D. Scott (ed), *Progress in Natural Resource Economics*, Oxford: Clarendon Press.

Sedjo, R.A. (1995), 'Forests: Conflicting Signals', in R. Bailey (ed), *The True State of the Planet*, New York: The Free Press.

Seneca, J.J. and M.K. Taussig (1984), *Environmental Economics*, Englewood Cliffs: Prentice-Hall.

Shogren, J.F., J.A. Herriges and R. Govinsdasamy (1993), 'Limits to Environmental Bonds', *Ecological Economics*, **8**, 109-133.

Simmons, I.G. (1993), *Environmental History: A Concise Introduction*, Oxford: Basil Blackwell Ltd.

Simon, J.L. (ed) (1995), *The State of Humanity*, Oxford: Basil Blackwell.

Simpson, R.D., R.A. Sedjo and J.W. Reid (1996) 'Valuing Biodiversity for Use in Pharmaceutical Research', *Journal of Political Economy*, **104**, 163-185.

Sinclair, W.F. (1991), 'Controlling Effluent Discharges from Canadian Pulp and Paper Manufacturers', *Canadian Public Policy/Analyse de Politique*, **17**

(1), 86-105.

Solbrig, O.T. (1992), 'Biodiversity: An Introduction', in O.T. Solbrig, H.M. van Emden and P.G.W.J. van Oordt (eds), *Biodiversity and Global Change*, Wallingford: CAB International, pp. 13-20.

Somerville, R.C.J. (1996), *The Forgiving Air: Understanding Environmental Change*, Berkeley, CA: University of California Press.

Spence, A.M. and M.L. Weitzman (1993), 'Regulatory Strategies for Pollution Control', in R. Dorfman and N.S. Dorfman (eds), *Economics and the Environment* (third edition), New York: Norton & Company, pp. 205-224.

Stern, D.I, M.S. Common and E.B. Barbier (1996), 'Economic Growth and Environmental Degradation: The Environmental Kuznets Curve and Sustainable Devlopment', *World Development*, **24** (7), 1151-1160.

Stevenson, G.G. (1991), *Common Property Economics - A General Theory and Land Use Application,* Cambridge: Cambridge University Press.

Swallow, B.M. and D.W. Bromley (1995), 'Institutions, Governance and Incentives in Common Property Regimes for African Rangelands', *Environmental and Resource Economics,* **6**, 99-118.

Swanson, T. (1993), 'Regulating Endangered Species', *Economic Policy,* **16**, 185-205.

Theeuwes, J. (1991), 'Regulation or Taxation', in D.J. Kraan and R.J. in't Veld (eds), *Environmental Protection: Public or Private Choice*, The Netherlands: Kluwer.

Thivierge, M. (1992), 'Gananoque's Experience with User Pay Waste Disposal', mimeo, presented at the Recycling Council of Ontario Conference, October 1992.

Thornton, R. (1987), *American Indian Holocaust and Survival: A Population History Since 1492*, Norman, Oklahoma: University of Oklahoma Press.

Tietenberg, T.H. (1994), *Environmental Economics and Policy*, New York: HarperCollins.

Tietenberg, T.H. (1995), 'Transferable Discharge Permits and Global Warming', in D.W. Bromley (ed), *The Handbook of Environmental Economics*, Oxford: Blackwell, pp. 317-352.

Tietenberg, T.H. (1996), *Environmental and Natural Resource Economics*, fourth edition, New York: HarperCollins.

Tinbergen, J. and R. Hueting (1992), 'GNP and Market Prices: Wrong Signals for Sustainable Economic Success that Mask Environmental Destruction', in R. Goodland, H.E. Daly and S. El Serafy (eds), *Population, Technology, and Lifestyle*, Washington, DC: Island Press, pp. 52-62.

Titus, J. (ed) (1986), *Effects of Changes in Stratospheric Ozone and Global Climate*, Washington, DC: Environmental Protection Agency.

Turner, R.K., D. Pearce and I. Bateman (1994), *Environmental Economics: An Elementary Introduction*, Hemel Hempstead: Harvester Wheatsheaf.

United Nations Environment Programme (UNEP) (1992), *Urban Air Pollution in Megacities of the World*, Oxford: Basil Blackwell.

United States Bureau of the Census (1996), http://www.census.gov./ipc/www/worldpop.html.

van Kooten, G.C. (1993), *Land Resource Economics and Sustainable Development: Economic Policies and the Common Good*, Vancouver, BC: University of British Columbia Press.

Vedeld, T. (1992), 'Local Institution-Building and Resource Management in the West African Sahel', *Forum for Developing Studies*, **1**, 23-50.

Wade, R. (1987), 'The Management of Common Property Resources', *Cambridge Journal of Economics*, **11**, 95-106.

Weber, P. (1994), 'Facing Limits in Oceanic Fisheries - Part I: Extent of the Problem and Policy Responses', *Natural Resources Forum*, **18**, 293-303.

Weitzman, M.L. (1993), 'What to Preserve? An Application of Diversity Theory to Crane Conservation', *Quarterly Journal of Economics,* **108**, 157-183.

Weyant, J.P. (1993), 'Costs of Reducing Global Carbon Emissions', *Journal of Economic Perspectives*, 7, 27-46.

Wilen, J.E. (1993), 'Enhancing Economic Analysis for Fishery Management: Discussion', *American Journal of Agricultural Economics*, **75**, 1198-1199.

Williams, J.D. and R.N. Nowak (1993), 'Vanishing Species in Our Own Backyard: Extinct Fish and Wildlife of the United States and Canada', in L. Kaufman and K. Mallory (eds), *The Last Extinction* (second edition), Cambridge, MA: The MIT Press, pp. 115-148.

Wohlfarter, R. (1965), *Die Besitz- und Ertagsstruktur der Tiroler Alp und Weidewirtschaft*, Innsbruck: Amt der Tiroler Landesregierung, Abteilung III d4, and Imst, Austria: Egger Druckerei.

World Bank (1992), *World Bank Development Report 1992: Development and the Environment*, Oxford: Oxford University Press.

World Bank (1994a), *World Bank Development Report: Infrastructure for Development*, Oxford: Oxford University Press.

World Bank (1994b), *World Tables 1994*, Baltimore: The Johns Hopkins University Press.

World Commission on Environment and Development (1987), *Our Common Future*, Oxford: Oxford University Press.

Yamamoto, T. (1995), 'Development of a Community-Based Fishery Management System in Japan', *Marine Resource Economics*, **10**, 21-34.

Index

182 Economic Rights and Environmental Wrongs